MW00377707

Rustic

Artistry for the Home

Rustic

Artistry for the Home

Written and photographed by

Ralph Kylloe

GIBBS·SMITH
PUBLISHER

Salt Lake City

First Edition

04 03 02 01 00   5 4 3 2 1

Published by
Gibbs Smith, Publisher
P.O. Box 667
Layton, Utah 84041

Orders: (1-800) 748-5439
Visit www.gibbs-smith.com

Design by FORTHGEAR, Inc.
Printed and bound in China

Library of Congress Cataloging-in-Publication Data

Kylloe, Ralph R.
    Rustic artistry for the home / written and
photographed by Ralph Kylloe.—1st ed.
        p. cm.
    ISBN 0-87905-966-4
    1. Interior decoration. 2. Decoration and
ornament, Rustic. 3. Country furniture. I. Title.
NK1986.R8 K96 2000
747—dc21
                                                    00-029706

For my daughter, Lindsey Nicole.
She is absolutely the thrill of my life.
May she achieve her own potential
and may she love rustic settings
as much as I do.

Contents

Preface viii

Beginnings 12
   Rustic Furniture Builders 16
   Styles 18

Adirondack or North Woods Style 20

Indiana Hickory Furniture 72

Rocky Mountain or Cowboy Style 88
   Antler & Horn Furnishings 148

California or West Coast Free Form . . . 158

Rustic from the Outside 172

Rustic from the Inside 200

Resources 244

Artists Index 253

Preface

This is my eighth book in seven years. Photographing and writing books does not get easier as the years go by. Homes are bigger today and are often built in remote and inaccessible places, so I have to travel farther and spend more time to finish what needs to be done. Nonetheless, not one part of my "job" is not enjoyable. The vast majority of people I have met have been incredibly friendly, open and encouraging. On several occasions people who have wanted me to see their homes have sent their private airplanes for my transport. Many of the owners have not only allowed my wife, our infant daughter and me to stay in their homes for extended periods, but they have also provided a vehicle, meals, servants, guides and other accommodations. I am overwhelmed at the generous hospitality, and I must say that it is quite thrilling to stay in a house that often costs in the tens of millions of dollars. We have become close friends with many of the owners of the homes that we have photographed.

An example of just how extraordinary these experiences can be was in September of 1999. We were photographing a home near Ennis, Montana. It was a good hour's drive down a lonely dirt road before we arrived at the complex. The place was an absolute Rocky Mountain wilderness at its finest. Once we settled in we worked for several hours, then in the evening drove to town for a meal. As we drove back to the home, we saw, by the light of a full moon, herds of elk, several moose, coyotes and other animals scurrying across the road. Back at the house we relaxed by a roaring fire and retired to the sound of coyotes in the distance. Around midnight we heard a commotion in the front yard. Coyotes had taken a deer, and their feasting and howling kept us up most of the night. We were not disappointed in the least by the noise. In the morning I wandered down to a small stone fishing cabin that was part of the complex and threw several grasshoppers into the pond. Schools of monster, two-foot rainbow trout attacked the insects. The entire setting was unforgettable.

Another exhilarating adventure took place in the fall of 1999. Furniture maker Michael Patrick arranged for me to photograph a remote ranch that was accessible only by private airplane.

It was a picture-perfect day when we took off for the twenty-five-minute flight. During the first part of the ride, I enjoyed a stunning view of the rolling hills around Cody and listened calmly to the small talk between Michael and the pilot. Then, near the edge of the Bear Tooth Range, the plane began to shudder violently. I sat white-knuckled in a state of near terror as the plane crossed over the pass, bouncing,

jolting, and shaking its way north. The jagged peaks below were so close that with just a bit of effort I was certain I could touch them.

After several more minutes the pilot pointed out the runway where he had every intention of landing. I was shocked to think he had landed a plane on that spot every day for the past seven years. And so we began our descent into the abyss. Absolute terror permeated every cell in my body. Jagged peaks, monstrous boulders and cliffs so steep that they were ignored by mountain goats, were close enough to touch. In time, a rock-strewn trail that had obviously been used by a horse-drawn wagon began to take shape. Full of mounds, dips and sagebrush, the runway slowly emerged; the end of the trail was coming fast. Finally, after my blood pressure had reached record levels, the plane touched the runway. And all the while Michael and the pilot chitchatted about local gossip. Within a hundred feet of a thousand-foot-drop-off cliff, the pilot whipped the plane around and taxied back to a barn, from where we took a short pickup trip to the compound.

The setting was as remote as it gets. Everything required to build each of the seven buildings had been flown in by helicopter over a two-year period. The entire facility was magnificent and extremely comfortable. The major buildings, created from reclaimed materials from nearby historical structures, were styled and furnished with exceptional vernacular furniture. Of course the views from all sides were extraordinary.

The flight back was far worse than the flight in. I made the profound mistake of keeping my eyes open as we hurtled at breakneck speed toward the drop-off at the end of the runway. The tiny six-passenger plane made it into the air within just a few feet of the cliff and bounced around like a leaf in a storm as Michael and the pilot resumed their conversation. I did not hear a word they said. The day is remembered as one of the most terror-filled days of my adult life. I would have rather had root canal work. But, alas, it was a fantastic ranch and I would do it again in a second.

I make all my own photographs. The agreement I have with the home owners is that I will never say where the house is or to whom it belongs, unless requested to do so by them. I have published hundreds of photos and have thousands of slides of rustic settings in my archives; maybe a hundred years from now they will be worth something. I also have an extensive collection of historical photos of rustic settings, gathered over the past two decades, and a vast accumulation of early records and advertising from many different historic rustic furniture companies. Hopefully, in years to come, the entire collection will find a home in a museum somewhere.

With the help of my wife, I try to make each photo a perfect still life. Balance, depth, lighting, telling a story, etcetera, are all concepts that are important to me. In general, we use only natural lighting, but occasionally we need to "fill-in" an area that needs a bit of help.

On occasion, I really do nothing more than push a few buttons. Yes, I have to be concerned with light, exposure, forms, and a hundred other things. Nevertheless, the real credit goes to the architects, rustic furniture builders, interior designers, and the creative spirit in all of us. Even so, I thoroughly enjoy the writing and the photography end of doing books. I really see what I do as art and find great fulfillment when I open a box of slides that have just been processed or redesign a restaurant in classic rustic style.

Both experienced and neophyte artists realize that there is nothing like art. The human spirit is elevated to new heights through artistic endeavors—and quality counts.

Many years ago I realized that rustic furniture was one of the really great art movements of the world. It had unprecedented historical connections but was significantly misunderstood and underappreciated. My sole effort throughout the past two decades has been to research, document and record the efforts of accomplished artists around the country (as well as make a living). I have often been told that my books and my rustic furniture business have led the way in making it popular. The truth is, I was fortunate to be exposed to such wonderful craftsmanship and furniture art.

Most of the rustic furniture makers I have listed in the resource section of my books have been very pleased to see an increase in business. Unfortunately, space dictates that I can list only a portion of the craftsmen who contact me. I am also certain, however, that there are many people around the country whom I have not met who also do extraordinary work. The truth is that the people whose work appears in my books have earned it. The world is a better place because of them. It has been an absolute thrill to get to know, on a very personal level, many of the great rustic artists around the country. I only wish that I had the talent and patience to do what they do.

This book focuses on rustic settings and rustic furnishings. Throughout the years many people have called me and commented that they want to collect as well as furnish their entire homes with original Ernest Stowe furniture. Stowe, who worked at the beginning of the 1900s, was the Adirondacks' most celebrated rustic furniture maker. Frankly, as an antiques dealer, I would like to have taken their money; but it is impossible to collect Stowe furniture because he only made a few pieces. Many people want to collect antique rustic furniture, but the availability and scarcity of such furnishings make their endeavors nearly impossible.

Consequently, the majority of this book focuses on the efforts of this country's greatest contemporary rustic artists. It also shows numerous antique items that will, hopefully, broaden the scope of the viewer's historic appreciation and record significant rustic pieces before they are lost to time.

I have included a section on the efforts of the Old Hickory Furniture Company because this one-hundred-year-old firm has had more influence on rustic style in America than any other single effort. I have included photos of a number of their rare historic pieces, as well as some of their contemporary offerings. Realistically, because of the longevity, size and scope of the Indiana hickory furniture movement, it is possible to collect many antique pieces.

For more than a year, I have worked closely with numerous people to complete this project. It would not have been possible to achieve without the help of John and Jo Ann Lefner, Margaret Grade, Brian Kelly, Barney and Susan Bellinger, Erin Bellinger, Peter Winter, Barbara and Frank Siepker, John Bennett, Lori Toledo, Chris Wager, Tom Welsh, Lester and Nan Santos, Mike and Virginia Patrick, Peter Dominick, Peter Torrance, Ron and Jean Shanor, Tom and Don Devlin, Doug Tedrow, Janice Smith, Bob Oestreicher, Marvin O'Dell, Phil Clausen, Dan Mack, Matt Madsen, Tim Duncan, Diane Cole-Ross, Randy Holden, Michael and Kim Cantanucci, Jeff Klembczyk, Jimmy and Lynda Covert, Cheryl Gallinger, Chris William and the Old Hickory Furniture Company, Diana Beattie, Terry and Sandy Winchell, Mike and Terry Griffin, Henry Caldwell, Graham Davis, Veronica Nemethy, Jerry and Jessica Farrell, Katheryn Kincannon, Crystal Farm, Dan MacPhail, Chip Kalleen, Thome George and Cloudbird, Bobby and Ginny Mason, Michael Hutton, Patty Fowler, Marvin Davis, Bill and Wendy Nolan, Jim Howard, John Gallis, David and Christie Garrett, Brent McGregor, Kara Mickaelson, John Mortensen, John and Wendy Starling, Nancy Simpkins, Cathy Klingstein, David and Margaret Devoe, Tom and Ceily Eustice, Melissa Greenauer, Lee Kern, Pete Imbs, Thea Marx, David Leuschen, Colleen and Glen Urkuhart, Gail and Jen Nace, Bo and Anna Polk, Page and Pearre Williams, Jon Foote, Pat and John Nolan, Colleen Boehmer, David M. Schwartz Architectural Services, Dan and Gayle Cook, Linda and Bud Mellon, and numerous others who are unmentioned. I personally thank all of you for your hospitality and generosity.

I want to offer profound gratitude to my publisher, Gibbs Smith, who lets me do just about whatever I want (as long as he approves of it beforehand!), and to my editor, Madge Baird. She definitely keeps me in line, is the quintessential professional and makes coherent sense out of my "ramblings." Thank you both.

Finally, I cannot speak highly enough of my wife, Michele. She runs my business, keeps our house going, styles many of the photographs, takes perfect care of our daughter and constantly supports me in my lifelong attempt to keep my head above water.

Beginnings

> " *If we all did the things
> we are capable of doing
> we would literally astound ourselves.*"
>
> —Thomas Edison

The uniqueness of both life and consciousness often evades us. The notion of our close connection to all other things, both organic and inorganic, is not something that most of us dwell upon. For instance, the molecules and the laws of nature that govern all things are exactly the same laws and molecules that exist in galaxies millions of light-years from us. We and all things are far more closely connected than we dare realize. There are only a few more than a hundred naturally occurring elements throughout the cosmos, and all living things share these in common; just a few of those elements include carbon, hydrogen, and oxygen. We are tied, for all time, to all other things in the cosmos.

As humans, we are often perplexed by our own behavior. Our inhumanity toward others troubles us deeply; yet, evolutionary biologists tell us that we behave as the laws of nature dictate. Our struggles against other forces demand that we behave in ways that perplex our souls and make us question the nature of ourselves as a species.

In the beginning we lived close to nature. As we evolved from tree dwellers to hunter/gatherers, we were very close to the essence and nature of the world into which we came. We had with us our tools of the hunt and we wore the skins of the beasts we slew. In early times, I believe—and native cultures throughout the world today behave in such a manner—we did not hunt for sport. We hunted for subsistence. We respected the life around us for what it was, and we took no more than what was needed.

In our caves and huts we surrounded ourselves with souvenirs of the hunt. We painted symbols on the walls of our dwellings with images of our daily activities. We had with us at all times our spears and arrows and fishing gear. At night we sat around campfires and spoke to each other of the day's thrills and disappointments. It is on these realities that the style of rustic is based today.

At the same time, living a rustic lifestyle has other, more meaningful, benefits.

The greatest battle each human will ever face is the unreasonable and clearly misunderstood battle for self-respect. In our early years we could see immediately the implications of our actions. Like all other species we knew what we needed to know in order to survive. We were a part of nature, not apart from it. We worked closely with each other. There were no fences or boundaries. The hazards were there but the challenges, and our ability to meet them, allowed us to see ourselves as capable, competent individuals.

Our connection with nature has been, in modern times, superseded by our ability and capacity to create a technological world that even as little as a hundred years ago, humans would have never thought possible.

And through our mazes of concrete, polymers, plastics, fiber optics, and Teflon™—all of which are quite extraordinary and incredibly beneficial to humanity—we have both insulated and isolated ourselves from a world of which we are so much a part.

My wife, our daughter and I live in the Adirondack Mountains. In our backyard, deer, moose, mountain lions, bear and numerous other animals frequent us. Quite frankly, I love all of them. When I am troubled, I frequently walk the trails behind my house and marvel at the solace inherent in the woods, where only natural sounds occur and peace prevails.

But our superficial observation of the woods is misleading. Moment by moment, millions of insects are killed and eaten by other insects and birds. Small mammals are overcome by larger ones, and the large, top-of-the-food-chain animals eat what they want when they want. The roots of trees fight violently for water and minerals, and the trees themselves battle for precious space and sunlight. It is a world filled with violence, cunning and strength. In reality, it is not a peaceful place.

As an academic I often struggle with the very essence of life. What caused cells to divide? What miraculous thing "willed" the desire and ability into every last ounce of protoplasm to adapt to its environment? What causes us to go on? In the face of the cosmos we are insignificant beings. The time we occupy on this planet is incredibly short. But in these truths I find strength and peace. Life does go on. Creatures of astounding beauty inhabit every last nook of the earth. Trees of utmost beauty call to the skies, consume the poisonous carbon dioxide emitted by us and, in turn, emit pure oxygen that allows us and all other creatures to survive. It is an elegant symbiosis.

However, there is more to trees and plants than we often acknowledge. It takes three acres of mature trees to make enough oxygen for one person

to breathe. They hold the earth in place and prevent erosion. They are the homes for untold millions of creatures. The colors of their leaves in the fall both thrill and fascinate us. And in the winter and spring their decaying leaves provide food for all kinds of flora. They are only good. They benefit every living thing.

Apart from the realities of biology there is the continuing fascination of the philosophical. It is the very nature of nature that thrills and fascinates us. Nature abounds with freedom. Phototropism, the actual growth of the tree or plant toward the sunlight, requires that plants move in ways that can only be called a dance. The twists and turns of branches create sensual forms that are ethereal in nature. And the gnarls and knots on the surface of trees speak of a freedom that humans long for in their daily lives.

Equally as important as the aesthetics of plant life, the process of growth and maturation of a single seed amongst millions of others that didn't survive captures my imagination and speaks volumes about the ability to live and thrive.

Some things are sacred to me. My most humbling moments have been when I have walked below the giant redwoods in California. Being among these trees is as close to a religious experience as I have had. Their immense size, spiraling toward the heavens, speaks silent words of sheer determination. They have withstood fires, plagues, and the desire of many humans to turn them into lumber. It is a sacrilege to cut them down. Fortunately, many of the old-growth trees have been set aside and will no doubt thrill future generations.

And, so, I find peace in the woods. And so do others.

Our world today, however, is an endless rhythm of commuting, work, computers and TV screens. Many of us, unfortunately, have become isolated from the world from which our species evolved. I call this the blight of over-civilization. Too much pavement, too much TV, and too much technological stress has taken its toll on many of us, and as a reaction, we long for a simpler existence filled with easy times and natural things. So we keep pets in our homes. We plant gardens and trees around our dwellings to keep us close to nature. We bring fresh-cut flowers—and even flowers made of linen and plastic—into our homes to remind us of the fields and prairies we once roamed. Nature, and our hunter/gatherer existence, is hard-wired into our brains. We need it, even once in awhile, to keep our wits together.

This is certainly not a new philosophy. The Romantics argued for it. Henry David Thoreau lived and argued for it, as did many others throughout recorded history. But it is, in light of the complexity of our society, a philosophy that might increase the quality of life for many in today's world.

Realistically, we will not change from our course of technology. Life is easier with gadgets. I, for one, love my computer (how did people write books without them?) and my telephone. I am astounded by the Hubble telescope and MRIs. I'm elated whenever I see the space shuttle blast off and I marvel to think that my voice is being bounced off a satellite and heard, just milliseconds later, in Europe. We are now living the future.

Fortunately, there is also a dramatic resurgence in the appreciation of the natural world. Interest in things rustic has grown progressively during the past decade. Log-home builders are busier than ever, and interior decorators are scrambling to find products to decorate these homes. Wilderness vacations are now the rage, and museums are including rustic items in their collections.

Not surprisingly, rustic furniture makers are basking in profound attention for their creations. Nurtured by a demanding public and a realization that a market exists, rustic furniture is finding its way into mainstream America.

Rustic furniture is interesting stuff. Not for the fainthearted, furniture of this kind retains all the inherent knots, twists, gnarls and grotesqueness that nature offers—the more exaggerated the better. Sometimes, the bark remains intact, permanently affixed to the wood just like it's supposed to be. No attempt is made to hide or disguise any of the natural elements associated with the branches, sticks, roots, and limbs that are used to construct and embellish the furniture.

Crafting rustic furniture, then, relies on tremendous artistic vision—vision to see what is already there, but to see it in a different light, a revised context.

Rustic Furniture Builders

Rustic furniture makers are a breed unto themselves. True entrepreneurs, they generally live outside of mainstream society. They are folk artists. Mostly without formal training in their field, they go against convention and rely on nature for designs and inspiration. Rustic builders do not go into the woods for a branch and saw it into a chair leg. Rather, nature tells them exactly what a branch or a root will be made into. The inherent form of the tree is honored and respected, and no attempt is made to shape something into something that was not intended to be. Approached this way, the integrity of nature itself is both honored and maintained.

A personal preference before I go on: In our society we have come to use the word *artist* in too casual a fashion. Just because someone can play a musical instrument or build a chair does not mean that the person is an artist. I can accept the words *guitar player* or *craftsperson,* but the term *artist* should be reserved for someone who goes way beyond the norm, who makes a significant innovation or contribution to the field; someone who is so accomplished at his or her craft that the quality and innovation of his/her efforts are instantly recognized.

As owner of a large rustic furniture gallery, I am questioned daily about rustic designs and practitioners. My files hold portfolios and photos from literally hundreds of aspiring rustic furniture makers all around the world. Realistically, the vast majority of people doing this sort of work are accomplished builders who are making a living (albeit "struggling along") doing what they love.

Most of the people who either write or visit my gallery are looking for inspiration for their next project. In general, I tell them two things: The first and most important is that nature itself is far more creative and inventive than humans will ever be. They should spend time just walking in the woods, looking at the shapes and forms of nature. I have challenged many individuals to take a magnifying glass, get down on hands and knees, and follow an insect around for an hour or so. Insects offer some of the finest, most innovative forms imaginable. Even a madman could never conceive of all the bizarre shapes, sizes and colors associated with insects. They are the pinnacle of creation. Existing on the planet for millions of years, they are an absolute miracle of innovation. *Leg length, overhang, balance, color, depth,* and *functional forms*—these terms of the art world are directly applicable to insects. Tom Benware, a carpenter who wanted to enter the rustic-furniture world, came by my place to talk about designs. I suggested he follow a daddy longlegs around for an hour and use the spider for inspiration for his furniture. Tom came back to my gallery a week later with a really great table based on his experience with the spider.

I also advise people to spend time at museums where extensive furniture collections are on display. It is important to understand historic and traditional forms and to recognize quality. It's also useful to understand why some pieces of furniture are residing there on display and others are sitting in secondhand-furniture stores.

Only a handful of people around the country are creating what I can honestly call rustic furniture art. It is this group of people who are very much in demand and making a good living in the business. They have demonstrated their ability to produce unique, high-quality, innovative artwork. It is they who have made contributions to the field and whose work is aggressively acquired by collectors around the country.

Making rustic furniture is hard work. People who do it do so because they love it and the lifestyle it affords them. I know of none who are getting rich from their efforts. Nonetheless, the vast majority of successful builders passionately love what they do.

The actual process of building rustic furniture is complicated. It is not as easy as pounding a few sticks together. Gathering materials is done in the winter when the sap is down. Anyone who has ever dug up a tree stump in winter knows that it is hard work. The materials are then either kiln-dried or stored for a year before they can be used. Further, one must have an exceptional grasp of power tools. (Just about every furniture builder I know has caused serious injury to himself with chop saws, planers or chain saws.) It is not uncommon for many of the great pieces to have been under construction for months. Once a piece is finished comes the difficult task of marketing it.

If one is new to rustic furniture building, I suggest a course in rustic furniture making. (Dan Mack and Clifton Monteith offer workshops.) Or an apprenticeship with an established builder would ease the learning curve.

I also want to say that every last human endeavor throughout all time has been copied. Because of human nature this is to be expected. There is, however, and will forever be, a significant difference between making an exact copy of something and being influenced by the efforts of others. Any accomplished builder who thinks that they will never have an influence on other builders is completely wrong. Imitation, as they say, is the

E GARDENERS CAMP, AT LAKEVIEW LODGE
BIG MOOSE LAKE N.Y.

greatest form of flattery. Similarities among the work of two builders should also be viewed as good because it forces them to continually strive for innovation and excellence in their work. Resting on one's laurels is a portent to failure.

At the same time, no one ever became famous or wealthy by making exact "knock-offs" of other people's furniture or artwork. Consequently, I can only encourage "start-up" builders to learn from those who have come before them but to seek their identity and their own creations.

Not surprisingly, the really great rustic artists today are talented in many fields. For instance, Barney Bellinger of Sampson Bog Studios is also an accomplished landscape painter and fly fisherman; Randy Holden plays the mandolin; and Lester Santos is an accomplished guitar maker and musician. Jerry Farrell traveled with a circus troupe in Alaska and played honky-tonk piano. Interests far beyond rustic furniture enrich the lives and vernacular of these artisans.

Most rustic furniture makers did not begin their careers building furniture. Chris Chapman, certainly the most respected leather worker today

(and winner of an award at the prestigious Western Design Conference), worked as a teacher in a maximum-security men's prison before gravitating to leather and woodworking. Clifton Monteith was in public relations in New York City. Barney Bellinger was a sign painter. Jim Howard was, and still is, a bush pilot working summers on the northwest coast of Vancouver Island. Phil Clausen was a farmer and real estate salesperson. Matt Madsen serviced equipment on the Alaska pipeline. Diane Cole-Ross has a degree in range sciences and worked as a "cowgirl."

The rustic furniture business is growing, and more and more people are trying their hand at making a living by building rustic furniture. For the past decade much of the high-quality work has been done by, just to name a few, Barney Bellinger, Matt Madsen, Phil Clausen, Lester Santos, Jerry Farrell, Dan Mack, Mike Patrick, Ron Shanor, Jack Leadley, Jimmy Covert, and others. New faces and a new generation have emerged and are making work that is quickly gaining appreciation and respect. John Gallis, John Bennett, Brian Kelly, Tom Benware, Thome George, Tom Welsh, Peter Winter, Lori Toledo, Tim Duncan, Chris Wager, Dan MacPhail, Doug and Janis Tedrow, John Omohundro, Al Boswell, Mike Hutton, Wayne Ignatuk, Tim Groth, and Andy Sanchez are a few whose work is gaining momentum.

Styles

Humans are a creative lot. We thrive when we have something to do. Psychologists and educators have different terms for the personal effects of our efforts: peak experiences, flow, maximum arousal, leisure and other labels are applicable when humans are intensely involved in an activity. Time stops and nothing else matters when our concentration is focused. The act of creating is reward in itself.

All people across the planet create. We all decorate. A prison inmate placing a photo of a loved one on a wall is not only an act of manipulation in an attempt to control his or her environment but also an act of creation. Anthropologists who have studied remote tribes in South America and Africa state that every culture they have visited both creates and decorates in some fashion. Besides personal expression, it is also a way of marking or announcing that a certain object is their own or was created by them.

While this analysis makes sense, at the same time there is no reason, logical or otherwise, for us to build sandcastles. It is done purely for the sake of creating. We love to create.

In the past, rustic furniture builders worked out of obligation and necessity. In the Adirondacks, gardeners, caretakers and guides often built furniture throughout the winter for their employers. Other craftspeople built furniture simply because they needed a dining room table and they could not afford to order one from the Sears, Roebuck catalog. And, in its simplest application, one needs only a hammer, a saw, a few nails and branches readily available in every backyard to create a piece of rustic furniture.

In time, many builders realized that they could make a living by selling rustic furniture to resorts, lodges and individual homeowners. Consequently, a cottage industry literally grew from the ground. At the same time, because of the simplicity of rustic furniture, many individuals recognized a chance to make a living during hard economic times. For instance, at least three different hickory furniture companies opened their doors in Indiana during the height of the depression in the early 1940s and succeeded in making a living for many years for themselves and numerous employees.

Nature, with its extraordinary creative forces, is the basis and inspiration for all designs. With just a touch of imagination, one can see that all furniture styles show nature's influence. For instance, tree roots influenced lamps created by Tiffany. Root bases from saplings directly inspired Queen

Classical southern corner settee created from either mountain laurel or rhododendron twigs, probably in the early 1900s. The twigs have been chip-carved in traditional southern style.

Anne and Chippendale feet. Inverted saplings inspired cabriole legs. Tree trunks spawned Duncan Phyfe tables.

It should be made clear, however, that Americans were not the inventors of rustic furniture. Examples of historical root-based tables, chairs, beds and other rustic furnishings have been found all across Europe and Asia. And many of the furniture makers who worked here in America were directly from Europe. For example, George Wilson, an Englishman, was a prolific furniture maker in the Adirondacks in the early 1900s. Another international figure who popularized rustic furniture in America was the

Reverend Ben Davis of Oteen, North Carolina (originally of Great Britain), the quintessential rustic furniture maker in the Appalachian regions of North Carolina. It is also well known that when Marjorie Merriweather Post built her now-famous Top Ridge great camp in the Adirondacks, she brought over some three hundred log builders from Scandinavia.

It is easy to delineate general origins of rustic furniture: Adirondackers and North Woods builders had birch bark, cedar and other hardwood trees; Rocky Mountain builders had lodgepole pine, juniper and antlers; builders from the South had massive rhododendron and mountain laurel saplings; in Florida, builders had cypress trees; West Coast builders had redwood trees; and builders in Indiana had vast stands of hickory.

Not only were materials different throughout the country but regional styles also evolved. North Woods builders (I use the term "North Woods" because similar furniture was built from Maine to Minnesota, and it is incorrect to call all such furniture "Adirondack") often applied sheets of birch bark on cases that were sometimes made from scrap wood. They were also known to apply tiny twigs in intricate patterns that became known as mosaic. Pieces were also built of cedar logs and branches.

Rocky Mountain, or "cowboy," builders often incorporated Indian motifs as well as extremely contorted wood burls or heavily twisted branches into their creations. They were also known to make use of massive elk or moose antlers.

Southern builders, usually from the Appalachian region, often applied chip-carved roots or branches onto their furniture. At the same time, both the Amish and the gypsies developed unique styles using the shoots of willow trees and small cedar trees. Rustic builders in Indiana utilized saplings from the vast stands of hickory that were prevalent in the area. So, realistically, in the spirit of traditional folk art, craftspeople simply went outside their doors, collected the necessary materials, and created furniture that is loved and admired today for its uniqueness, simplicity and individuality.

Hundreds of wine-bottle corks are inlaid into this birch-bark sideboard—
appropriate since the room is actually the wine cellar at the Lake Placid
Lodge. Guests at this Chateau Relais resort often utilize the room for private
parties and dinners. The sideboard was created by owner David Garrett.

Adirondack

or North Woods Style

When Americans think of rustic furniture, they generally think of the Adirondacks.

It has been surprising to listen to many people over the years talk about western, twig, or Indiana hickory furniture as Adirondack. It seems that almost anything that has bark on it is thought to be Adirondack.

Nonetheless, Adirondack furniture is typically made from cedar, birch, maple or other woods found in the Adirondack region of upstate New York. Specifically, Adirondack furniture was often adorned with mosaic twig work or covered with birch bark.

In truth, the exact types and styles of both furniture and architectural structures were made in the Adirondacks and have been found throughout the North Woods regions, from Maine to Minnesota.

Apart from these geographic realities, the Adirondacks really were the most visible of the rustic regions in North America. The great camps and the entire rustic movement were financed by the most visible and influential families in America. Mega-wealthy people who resided mostly in New York built some of the most remarkable architectural structures in the country. And in these homes they placed some of the most innovative rustic furnishings ever created.

Today rustic furniture making in the Adirondacks represents the upper end of the movement, enjoying brisk business and significant innovation and powered by the creative genius of a few exceptionally talented artists. High-quality furniture from the Adirondacks is finding its way into homes in California, Wyoming, Colorado, Montana, the Carolinas and many other regions of the country. Even traditional homes with white walls are boasting Adirondack furniture for upscale settings. Further, furniture styles typically thought to be Adirondack are being created by other builders around the country. For instance, the Old Hickory Furniture Company now adorns some of its furniture with birch bark. Builders in the Rocky Mountain region are also featuring birch bark and intricate mosaic patterns in their creations.

Consumers are finding that the once-"grotesque and uncomfortable-looking stick furniture" is really quite comfortable, functional and aesthetically pleasing—and still significantly underpriced.

Door hinge detail, below.

Door pull detail, right.

Both by Randy Holden.

Classic Nemethy Adirondack water scene in an extended palette is complete with frame adorned with acorns and other organic material.

Perhaps the most innovative piece of Adirondack furniture of the decade, the interior of this extraordinary armoire is replete with numerous drawers and cubbyholes. Randy Holden also created several innovative hinges, doorknobs and hidden lights.

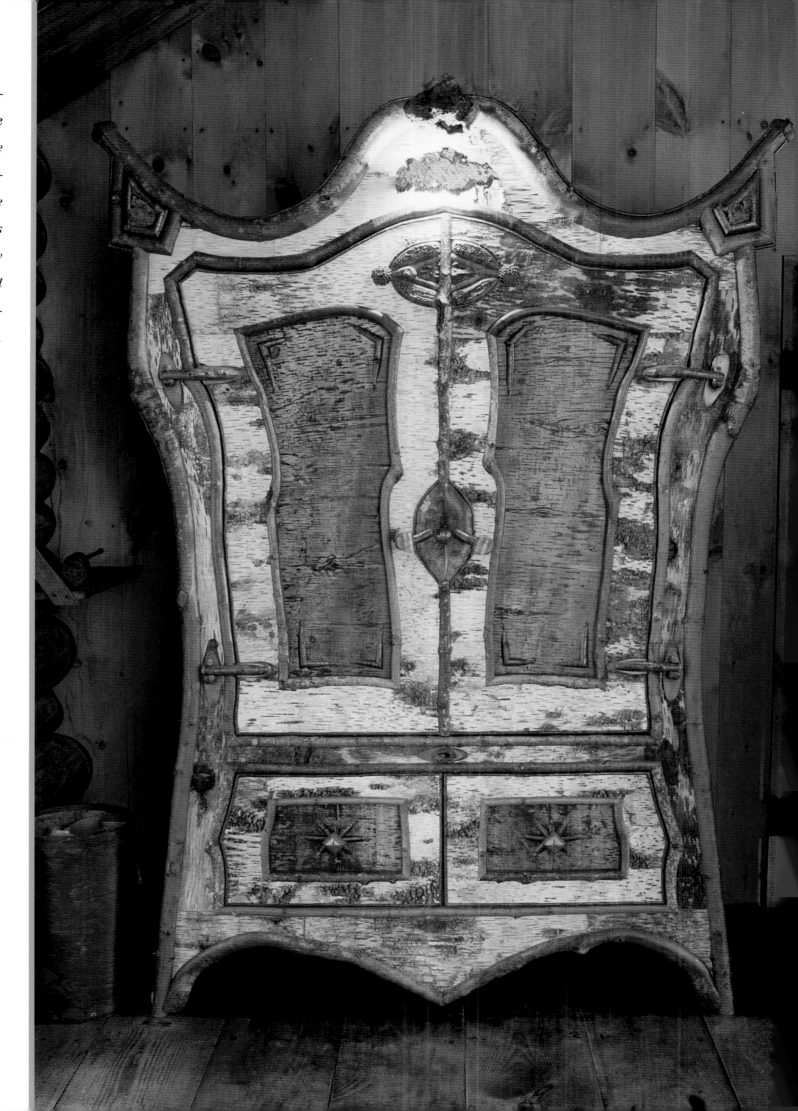

A small desk by Brian Kelly graces the entry-way of a cabin at the Lake Placid Lodge.

John Champney built this mosaic bureau in the 1930s. The room that houses the bureau and other Champney furniture is completely covered with birch bark.

Detail of a painting on a fly-tying desk by Barney Bellinger. Bellinger's artwork is surpassed only by his furniture.

At the request of the owner, Peter Winter covered this antique cupboard with birch bark and twigs. In a beautiful lakeside home in Lake George, New York, it houses an extensive collection of Adirondack collectibles.

This desk for fly tying was made by Barney Bellinger of Sampson Bog Studio. One of numerous innovative designs created by Bellinger, the desk resides in a lakeside home in the northern Adirondacks. Being avid fly fishermen, Barney and his wife Susan, who also works on the furniture, often incorporate fishing relics into their pieces.

This wardrobe was built by Stephen Chisholm of Vermont. The doors and other dimensional wood are spalted tiger maple. The burls are cherry, as are the handmade door hinges.

Although found in California, this antique white birch-bark dressing table was probably made in the East around the turn of the century. The piece now rests in a beautiful Wyoming ranch surrounded by Native American collectibles.

The dark bark that covers this diminutive cupboard by Peter Winter is the reverse side of white birch bark. The top is bird's-eye maple.

HUNTING
OR
TRESPASSING
ON THESE GROUNDS
PROHIBITED
UNDER PENALTY OF THE LAW

A work space in this Adirondack home is filled with rustic acces-

sories, including a collection of antique birds, pack baskets, Old

Hickory furniture, nets, paddles and other items.

This combination tall-case

clock and humidor was created by

Adirondack builder Jim Howard.

An exquisite armchair by
Adirondack builder Tom Welsh.
The back panels are cut from oak.
The single-panel, hand-carved seat
provides comfort and stability to
the chair. The posts and rungs are
kiln-dried yellow birch. The arms
are naturally shed antlers from
red stag deer. Tom also makes side
chairs of the same materials.

Doug Francis made this

contemporary slab-back chair.

Armchair and stump-based table by Mike Kuba.

Painting and frame
by Veronica Nemethy.

This collection of antique bird's-eye maple, tiger maple, and cherry canoe paddles hangs on a wall of the author's Adirondack home.

Peter Winter created this extraordinary breakfront. Complete with bird's-eye-maple shelves, the cupboard maintains a subtle art nouveau influence. The floor lamps were created by Randy Holden.

Detail of a moose painting by Barney Bellinger.

This small entertainment center, in classical Adirondack style, is covered with birch bark and hand-carved fish. The center was completed by Jim Schreiner.

This classic Adirondack cupboard was built by Peter Winter. United Crafts designed the tableware.

This intricate entertainment center, although originating in Montana, was designed with classical Adirondack mosaic twig inlay. The case for the piece was created from antique barn boards.

The small corner cupboard was built in Michigan. Note the log cabin and the mountain scene inlaid with twigs in the lower doors.

Peeled table by Douglas Francis of Aurora Rustics.

An ornate Adirondack sideboard, crafted by Randy Holden, is a handsome focal point in its contemporary setting.

An intricate hall table by
Barney Bellinger blends well into
this setting of rocks and wood.

This classic sofa table was created in
traditional Adirondack style by Peter
Winter. The suspended spheres were
created from lodgepole pine burls.

Tom Benware created this classic cupboard. The shelves are made of highly figured tiger maple.

The large sideboard, snowshoe sconces, and back mirror are all by Barney Bellinger. The chairs are by the Old Hickory Furniture Company.

The Adirondack bedroom
setting was constructed
by Peter Torrance.
The bed was built of
bark-off cedar logs.

Chest by Barney Bellinger. From his humble beginnings as a sign painter, Bellinger has come to be the most sought-after rustic builder in the country. His creativity and innovations lead the field.

Oil painting by Barney Bellinger.

This exceptionally detailed painting, of a Lake George scene, and its frame were created by artist Veronica Nemethy. The sideboard in classic Adirondack style was made by Chris Wager.

A classic rustic bureau adorned with twigs enhances the ambience of a bedroom in the Adirondack Park.

This yellow birch-bark bed occupies a cabin at the Lake Placid Lodge. The walls have been lined and trimmed with white birch bark and birch and cedar trees. Jim Lanthier and Jim Howard of Tupper Lake, New York, created the bed and cabin.

Red bedding and curtains add a sense of drama to this rustic setting, which includes an ornate root mirror by Jerry Farrell and a birch bed by Dennis Smith.

Barney Bellinger's art studio is a unique assemblage of artist's
supplies, works in progress, and fishing memorabilia.

*Internationally known artist
Veronica Nemethy began working
with Adirondack settings in the late
1990s. Not only does she paint but
she builds the frames as well.*

Highly detailed settee, vintage 1900–1910. One of four pieces residing in an isolated lakeside cabin in the Adirondack Park, it was constructed of locally cut cedar.

A matching sideboard to the settee (facing), the set remains in the exact spot where it was placed by the original owner and builder of the house around the 1900s. The uniqueness and intricacy of the set make the four pieces extremely rare and historically significant. The builder's identity, at this writing, is unknown.

Table detail, Adirondack Park.

47

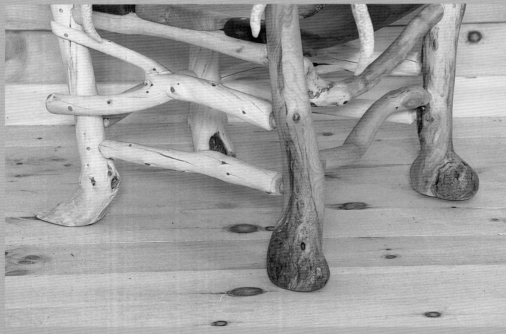

This ideal dining room setting, designed for a contemporary lakeside home in the Adirondack Park, includes a dining table and buffet by Peter Winter and chairs designed by the author and built by Old Hickory Furniture of Shelbyville, Indiana.

Queen Anne legs were inspired by the shape of tree-root bases, as can be seen on this rustic chair made in the Adirondacks.

This stunning table is nine by four feet with a solid cherry top and a base constructed of three large yellow birch roots. The built-in cabinets are faced with white birch bark. Barney Bellinger was the furniture artisan.

This stump-based Adirondack table fits pleasingly with designer fabrics, bountiful bouquets of flowers and traditional upholstered furniture.

Although this armchair was created using rhododendron roots, it falls into the North Woods tradition. Created by rustic artist Jerry Farrell, the chair is surprisingly comfortable.

Artist Michael Hutton of Illinois built this settee from yellow willow. He is perhaps the most innovative artist working in this form of rustic furnishings, creating a wide range of designs and patterns that he applies to settees, tables and cupboards.

The author designed the setting, built the massive tree bed, and decorated this cabin for the Lake Placid Lodge. Called "Owl's Head," the cabin itself was built in the 1920s and is part of a series of unique cabins available to the public.

This stump-based table is balanced by a rock on which the tree had grown for the duration of its life. Doug Francis made the table.

The home of the author includes
extensive collections of Adirondack-
related accessories, including antique
bird's-eye-maple paddles, creels, pack
baskets and other items. The cupboard
is by Barney Bellinger.

Peter Winter designed and constructed
this bed for the Lake Placid Lodge. Built
of yellow birch, the bed also maintains a
panel of contrasting white birch bark.

A unique rustic staircase makes a statement in the author's home. The stringers, stairs, and structural center beam are all red pine. The newel posts were created from the trunks of apple trees cut years before the staircase was made. Oak banisters came from trees cut on the property when the house was built. The antlers are caribou.

This designer log home in the Adirondacks
is a classic example of how traditional
Adirondack furniture blends tastefully with
well-chosen fabrics and upholstered pieces.

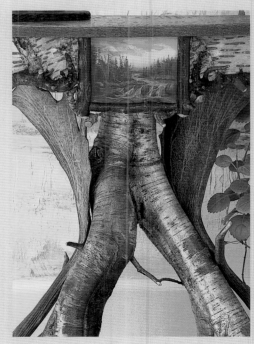

Bellinger's understanding of
form and colors has put him
at the top of Adirondack builders.

A mosaic twig pattern and small inlaid rocks embellish the top of a small root stand created by Barney Bellinger.

Small table and wall cabinet by John Bennett.

Musings on a daddy longlegs inspired this stand by Tom Benware. The hammered-copper lamp is by Michael Adams.

The yellow birch-bark bed is by Adirondack builder Barney Bellinger of Sampson Bog Studio.

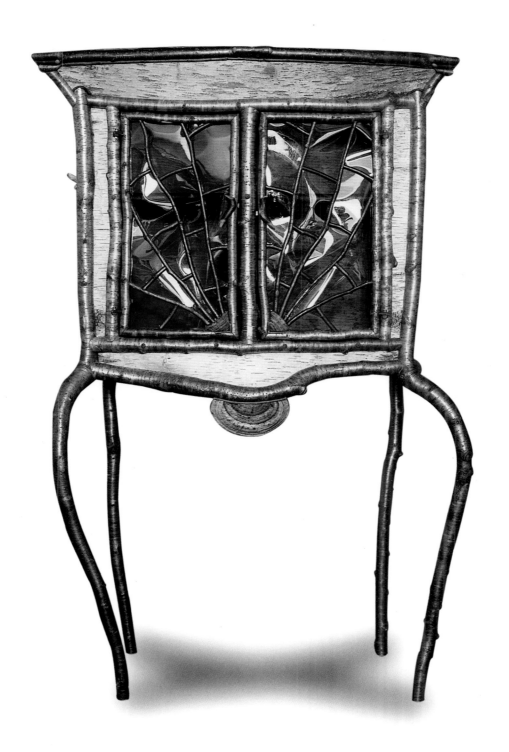

Cabriole legs were the invention of nature and were adapted for human use. Spider webs were the influence for the design on the front doors, which are lined with mica. Cupboard by Randy Holden.

57

Driftwood floor mirror by rustic artist Judd Weisberg.

The cupboard, in a cabin at the Lake Placid
Lodge, was created by Lionel Maurier.

Detail of a painting by Barney Bellinger.

Barney Bellinger created this yellow birch stump-based table with a tiger-maple top.

This ornate sofa table was created by John Bennett, who hand-carves and paints butterflies, moths and other winged creatures for adornment. Lori Toledo created the mirror and Tom Benware built the table lamp.

A table by Barney Bellinger has legs of fallow deer antlers and is adorned with one of Bellinger's classic Adirondack paintings. On the table sits an original Handel lamp. Bellinger also made the mirror behind the lamp.

Perhaps the most unique and original piece of rustic furniture ever made, this sideboard is the creation of rustic artist Randy Holden. Adorned with acorns, pinecones, and soapstones, this piece is a marvel of innovation and artistic interpretation.

An original Ernest Stowe mirror made in the early 1900s hangs over a 1930s Earl Rector table. A collection of original birch-bark frames adds to the setting in the author's dining room.

Randy Holden, creator of this unique bureau, is known for creating forms that are a significant innovation in the field of American furnishings. His attention to detail and his inclusion of minute parts of organic material, including pinecones, acorns and such, make his furniture highly collectible.

Barney Bellinger of Sampson Bog Studios created this one-of-a-kind cupboard, including the painted scenes on the doors. The piece was covered with white birch bark and trimmed with yellow birch saplings. The top crest is made from fallow-deer antlers.

Jim Howard constructed this elaborate Adirondack cupboard. Jim is a bush pilot who works off Vancouver Island during the summers and creates rustic furniture during the long, cold winter months in the Adirondacks.

Brian Kelly created this unique drop-front secretary. The exposed dimensional wood is spalted birch.

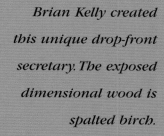

Brian Kelly of Lake George, New York, designed and constructed this drop-front desk that also acts as a telephone stand in the entryway where it resides.

Nemethy incorporated not only twigs and acorns but also sand
and stones in this innovative frame for her painting.

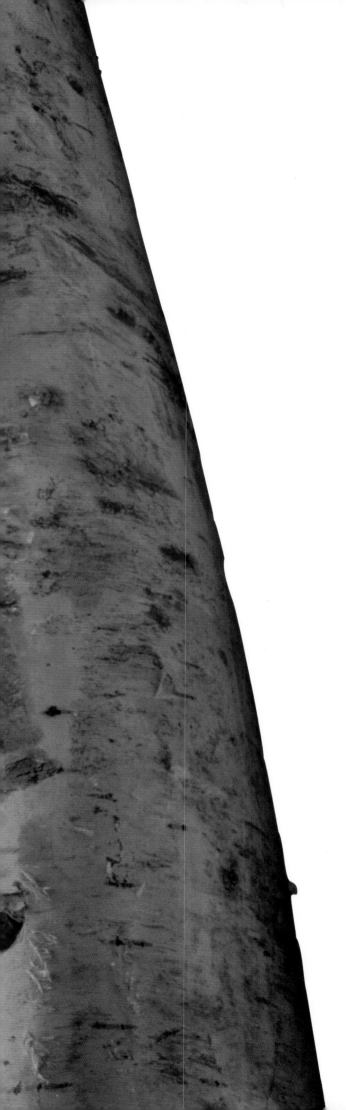

*This small rustic frame and
fish painting were made by
ten-year-old Erin Bellinger,
daughter of Barney and Susan.*

*Maple-and-cherry settee
by Stephen Chisholm.*

This unusual piece of hanging artwork by Barney Bellinger was created out of an antique canoe seat, guide-boat oars, oarlocks, light fixtures, bobbers, and roots. A classic Bellinger oil painting takes the center spot.

Adirondack artist Jerry Farrell made this tall-case clock. Jessica Farrell painted the clock face and door panel.

Michael Hutton built the settee and table at his workshop. His attention to detail, as well as his creative interpretation of rustic scenes, offers a fresh look within the realm of North American rustic furniture.

In the corner of the Bellinger household stands this classic Sampson Bog root stand. Adorned with a painting, the stand was made from the trunk and roots of a yellow birch tree.

Bellinger has added mosaic twig work, a clock, antlers, bark, oars, and a painting to what could have been an ordinary canoe bookshelf. That's his style—each piece is one of a kind.

This sofa was made by Randy Holden, certainly one of
the most creative individuals working within the
rustic furniture medium. He creates naturally inspired
furnishings in the classic Adirondack tradition.

Adirondack rustic builder Tom Benware created this sideboard.
The top was finished with highly figured tiger maple. The back
was adorned with a platform fungus.

*A pair of contemporary Old Hickory "Grove Park Inn" armchairs allow
the chef at this Adirondack home to relax for a few minutes and enjoy
the fire as well as the aromas from his culinary creations.*

Indiana

Hickory Furniture

No one movement or style of rustic furniture had more visibility or influence on the rustic market than that of the rustic furniture from Indiana.

Ten different manufacturers, beginning in the late 1890s, produced tens of thousands of pieces from hickory saplings that grew in vast stands in Indiana. And no company had more influence on the styles and visibility surrounding the movement than did the Old Hickory Chair Company in Martinsville, Indiana.

The hickory movement had its beginnings in the last quarter of the 1800s, when Billy Richardson of nearby Morgantown, Indiana, made hoop chairs and tables out of hickory saplings, loaded them onto a horse-drawn wagon, and sold his products at the farmers' market in Martinsville.

Within a few years, a small factory opened its doors in an abandoned church in Martinsville. The company was first owned by the Wood family of Martinsville and was later purchased by E. L. Brown and Ralph Barrett. During its early years, the company changed hands several times, until it was purchased in 1908 by William H. Patton, whose family retained ownership of the firm until the 1960s. Initially Old Hickory sold furniture to numerous health spas that had opened their doors in Martinsville because of the mineral water springs plentiful in the area. Visitors to the city were charmed by Old Hickory furniture, and many returned home with chairs for their own front porches. It is also known that Charles Limbert, a well-known Arts & Crafts designer, sold Old Hickory through his retail stores. Gustav Stickley also utilized Old Hickory furniture in many of his Craftsman bungalows that were being built around the country.

The Old Hickory Chair Company changed its name to the Old Hickory Furniture Company in 1921 to reflect the expanding number of products it was offering. In 1925, for example, the Old Hickory catalog offered 148 different pieces of furniture that included chairs, bureaus, gliders, beds and numerous other products.

In the 1930s, and possibly earlier, the company began applying to their furniture a small, dime-sized brass tag that read "Genuine Old Hickory, Bruce Preserved, Martinsville, Ind." A number embossed in the center of the tag indicated the year the piece was manufactured.

Old Hickory offered a line of traditional woven-seat and -back furniture in the 1940s. At this time, they applied a strip of oak to the front of the seat to protect legs and women's hosiery from rough edges of the rattan. The strip on the front seat is just one of many indicators that can date older pieces of hickory furniture.

Throughout its many years, the company offered different styles, including pieces designed by noted forties designer Russell Wright. Unfortunately, the Wright pieces failed to capture the imagination of the public and were quickly dropped from Old Hickory. The forms were considered too streamlined and did not live up to the ruggedness for which Old Hickory was known.

At its height Old Hickory produced two thousand pieces of furniture a week and sent boxcars of rustic furniture to every state on a daily basis.

Today historical pieces of Old Hickory can be seen at the Old Faithful Inn in Yellowstone National Park and numerous other state and national parks around the country.

Rustic furniture in the 1950s lost a significant share of the market to chairs made of both aluminum and plastic. During that period the remaining hickory furniture companies closed their doors and Old Hickory itself was forced to offer a traditional line of motel furniture to survive the times. But today the Old Hickory Furniture Company is alive and well. Presently located in Shelbyville, Indiana, it continues to manufacture pieces from its historical line of rustic hickory furniture as well as custom rustic pieces created by designers from all over the world. Places that are utilizing contemporary Old Hickory furniture include such well-known facilities as Disneyland and the Rainforest Café.

Old Hickory was not without its competitors during the twentieth century, and other towns in Indiana, including Laporte, Bedford, Jasper, Colfax, and Columbus, were homes to hickory-furniture companies. No other company, however, had the visibility, the designs, and the production capability of Old Hickory.

The Old Hickory corner cupboard is the home of numerous antique trophies. The chip-carved table was done by the Reverend Ben Davis in the 1930s. The mosaic table from the early 1900s came from Maine.

Signed on the bottom of the seat, the settee was purchased in the 1930s from the Indiana Willow Products Company of Martinsville, Indiana. Rustic collectibles and other hickory furniture complete the setting. The Willow Company changed its name to the Indiana Hickory Furniture Company and was a competitor to the Old Hickory firm.

This setting is the new "Mr. Brown's Pub" at the Sagamore Resort in Bolton Landing, New York. The author redesigned the facility, constructed the setting and used furniture from the Old Hickory Furniture Company as well as antler chandeliers and Adirondack memorabilia to create a wonderful rustic setting that guests and locals enjoy.

Heavily adorned with hickory spindles, this Old Hickory couch first appeared in the 1931 catalog and is a favorite with Arts & Crafts collectors. The Old Hickory floor lamps and table lamps are complete with antique mica shades. The tall-case clock was made at the Rustic Hickory Furniture Company in the 1920s.

This unique Old Hickory bureau, the only such bureau to be found, was a custom order in 1910. The woven material in the drawers and sides is indicative of very early designs and products from Old Hickory.

Both old and new pieces of hickory furniture grace this front porch in Montana. Today, hickory furniture is shipped to every state in the country and used in both residential and commercial settings.

The Crossed Sabres Ranch, built in the 1930s and located just outside the east entrance to Yellowstone National Park, boasts furniture that was original to the setting.

A lakeside porch in the Adirondacks is complete with original furniture from the Old Hickory Furniture Company. On rainy days the furniture is wisely pulled into a covered area.

This corner cupboard first appeared in the Old Hickory catalog in 1931. Made of oak and hickory saplings, its small size allows it to be used in a variety of rustic settings.

An antique deer-antler chandelier sheds light over an Old Hickory dining set in a home on the shores of Lake George, New York.

The Fisherman's Cabin at Mankas Inverness Lodge in Inverness, California, offers extraordinary comfort, inviting fireplaces, hot tubs, four-star dining and an impressive collection of antique Old Hickory furniture in just about every room.

*A very rare teacart and high chair made by Old Hickory in the 1930s
are both in mint condition and have aged to a rich brown patina.*

This armchair and table were completed at Old Hickory in the 1930s. The full wraparound rattan weaving is a signature of high-quality pieces.

*In pristine condition, this "senior glider" first appeared in the Old
Hickory catalogue in the late 1920s. The seat and back are woven
with the outer bark of the rattan plant imported from both Germany
and the Far East. The setting is a front porch in the Adirondacks.*

This settee was signed "Indiana Willow Products Company." The company was started by former employees of the Old Hickory Furniture Company in 1937 and closed its doors in 1963. A collection of antique creels and fish rests on the wall behind the settee.

Rare Windsor-style Old Hickory chairs first appeared in the 1931 catalog. The round table is also Old Hickory.

The varying colors inherent in juniper make it a favorite of builders and decorators alike. This massive king-size bed was built by Rocky Fork Juniper.

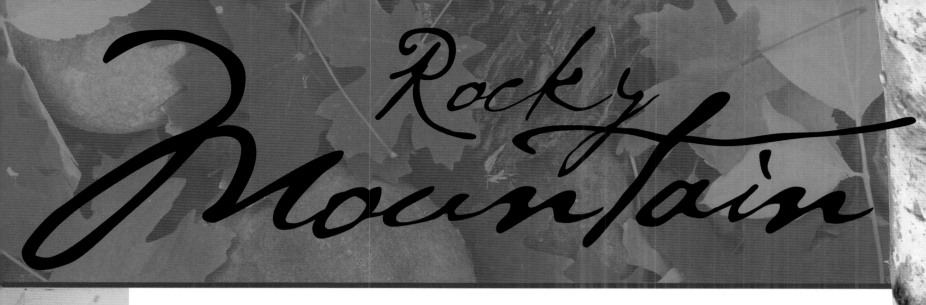

Rocky Mountain
or Cowboy Style

*Of interest to rustic furniture makers in the
Rocky Mountain region are the indigenous
growths of lodgepole pines and juniper trees,
as well as the abundance of antlers.*

Traditionally, rustic furniture makers in the Rocky Mountain region are, and have been, profoundly influenced by the Native American cultures, which had both a profound respect for and a deep connection to the land on which they lived. The presence of their gods and spirit world, which were intertwined with their daily lives, is evident in many Native American artifacts. The people took notice of natural patterns and forms, and incorporated those ideas into their artwork. They also used natural colors that were in harmony with the world in which they lived.

So pervasive and respected are the Native American arts that just about all of the western rustic furniture makers incorporate Indian motifs, symbols, patterns, or artifacts into their works.

Like much of the early rustic furniture in America, the vast majority of western rustic pieces from the early 1900s, as well as their makers' histories, have been lost to the ravages of time. Fortunately, prime examples of early 1920s and 1930s rustic pieces still exist and are treasured by their owners.

Without a doubt, the earliest known American rustic works are the Texas horn chairs that became popular in the late Victorian period and early twentieth century. However, during the 1920s, builders in the area of Jackson, Wyoming, experimented with and created a variety of innovative forms, utilizing lodgepole pine burls and elk antlers that were extraordinarily plentiful in their area. John Wurtz created many wonderful antler chairs during this time period. Other individuals, including Chet Woodward, Otto and Albert Nelson, George Rathe, Joe and Max Kudar, and Jack and Bob Kranenberg, were also instrumental in creating rustic furniture, some examples of which survive today.

A number of small dude ranches still in operation today are replete with prime examples of historic western, or "cowboy," furniture.

Certainly the most prolific, influential, and innovative character working within the medium of rustic furniture was Thomas Canada Molesworth, who started the Shoshone Furniture Company in the 1930s in Cody, Wyoming. Today his pieces command small fortunes at auctions. His style has also influenced just about every rustic furniture maker working in the Rocky Mountain cowboy style.

The Chippendale-style lodgepole pine chairs by Don King pair comfortably with the small cabinet in the center by Diane Cole-Ross. Working in the historical style of North Carolina artist the Reverend Ben Davis, Diane has created several distinctive pieces that employ chip carving on the applied twigs.

This contoured juniper floor lamp was built by the artists at Rocky Fork Juniper. Co-owner Peter Imbs makes the lamp shades by hand.

The burled lodgepole pine stringer and support pole for the balcony and staircase are beautifully accented by a juniper banister and railings.

Located in an extraordinary home in Aspen, Colorado, this leather set and related furnishings blend naturally into the log-cabin setting.

This contemporary setting is enhanced by the inclusion of a burled mantel, leather furniture, antler accessories, and Indian baskets. The setting was designed by Gallinger-Trauner Designs, Inc., of Wilson, Wyoming.

Furniture entrepreneur Thomas Molesworth invented a classic style in the 1930s with his leather-and-weavings pieces. The Molesworth furniture, along with the Native American artifacts, paintings and hickory furniture, are all of the period.

Leather furnishings, original antique paintings, a warmly inviting fireplace, and a telescope to watch the wildlife in the lower pasture—all the makings of a classic Rocky Mountain interior.

A breakfront cabinet by Ron Shanor of Cody, Wyoming, has a

stained-glass door in the center. The drawer pulls are made of antler.

A designer of leather creations, such as this armoire, for rustic settings,

Chris Chapman is the recipient of numerous design awards and is widely

regarded as the most accomplished leather worker in the country.

This hefty rocker blends well with the juniper banister and railings.

The artists at Rocky Fork Juniper created this vanity from select pieces of juniper.

Original Thomas Molesworth furniture is surrounded by other period decorative accessories. Navajo rugs paired with Molesworth pieces evoke a traditional western ranch style.

Rooms designed with rich textiles, leather, and lush greenery are comfortable as well as striking. The living room set is by Crystal Farm.

Overlooking the Snake River in Wyoming, this designer home is a marvelous fusion of rustic and traditional contemporary furnishings.

This inspirational settee was designed and built by rustic artist Lester Santos of Cody, Wyoming. Jimmy Covert, also of Cody, made the settee in the background.

Part of a set of rustic out-door chairs presently used on a patio in Colorado.

This dining room set, created by New West, features a cupboard with an original hand-painted western scene on its front doors. The base of the table is a huge lodgepole pine burl. Antique Native American baskets round out the setting.

Someone with innovative vision turned an old branch from the property into a unique door handle.

This set of tall bar stools are by John Gallis, who is known for his innovative designs and quality workmanship. Side chair (against the wall) by Lester Santos.

Greg Race of Colorado created this diminutive breakfast set.

A dining room set and corner cupboard are by Mike Patrick of New West. An original George Innes painting overlooks the dining area. The large Navajo rug probably dates from the 1930s.

This kitchen setting was completed with aged barn wood in a home built by Yellowstone Traditions in Montana.

Contemporary moose-antler armchair by the craftsmen of New West in Cody, Wyoming.

The sleek lines and minimalist
appearance give a modernist appeal
to this settee by John Gallis.

This contemporary log-home setting is
emboldened with colorful traditional furniture.

Side panels hand-carved with the likeness of Buffalo Bill Cody enhance a small sideboard by New West.

Rustic artist Jimmy Covert made this bedside table. The bear was hand-carved by Rodney Skenandore.

This unique chair was built by Montana artist John Omohundro, who works with a variety of woods.

Maintaining an "Alice in Wonderland" look, this innovative cupboard was designed and crafted by rustic artist Ron Shanor.

A modernistic mesquite sideboard made its way from the workshop of Tim Mowry in Annapolis, Maryland, to a Rocky Mountain home. The handles are wrought iron wrapped with leather. The rough edge on the top adds to its rustic character.

Rocky Fork Juniper in Red Lodge, Montana, turned out this juniper bedside table and table lamp.

Small table by New West.

A close-up shows how the colors of leather, lodgepole burls, and Native American carpets blend to create warm, striking hues.

A juniper table base is open to view through the coffee table's glass top.

This feminine settee was made by Jean Shanor. The burled lodgepole pine is covered with decorated leather.

John Gallis used juniper for the legs and drawer pulls of this table. The drawer fronts are Australian lace wood and the top is a solid walnut slab.

Working in the style of the Reverend Ben Davis, Doug and Janis Tedrow created this sideboard, complete with chip-carved molding. The piece rests between a pair of armchairs by early-twentieth-century architects and designers Greene & Greene.

Made from twisted juniper, these comfortable chairs by rustic artist Lester Santos are covered with leather. A collection of antique Adirondack pack baskets, snowshoes and canoe paddles complete the setting.

A table created from locally cut branches and a thick barn-board top becomes a focal point of the room.

Artistically made, these classic chairs by Tim Groth provide their owner with a comfortable setting, overlooking the Snake River in Wyoming.

A rustic staircase combines with horn and antler furnishings for an upscale look in a traditional contemporary setting.

This massive fireplace reaches nearly three stories high. The Morris chairs are by Stickley. New West created the leather-covered sofas.

Cushions on top of the plank seats make these chairs comfortable for patio seating on a Colorado Rocky Mountain evening.

A slab from a tree makes an interesting stair step.

In a back hallway of a Montana home is this charming staircase. The newel posts and banister were made from poles cut on the owner's property. Deer antlers embellish the design.

Certainly one of the most original rustic pieces ever created, this cupboard by Doug and Janis Tedrow of Wood River Rustics incorporates a number of materials, including sagebrush and willow as well as moose, elk, and deer antlers. The piece displays antelope and buffalo horns, a snapping-turtle shell, a rattle from a rattlesnake, and feathers from a wild turkey. It also features extensive beadwork.

Detail of cupboard by Doug and Janis Tedrow.

Detail of cupboard by Doug and Janis Tedrow.

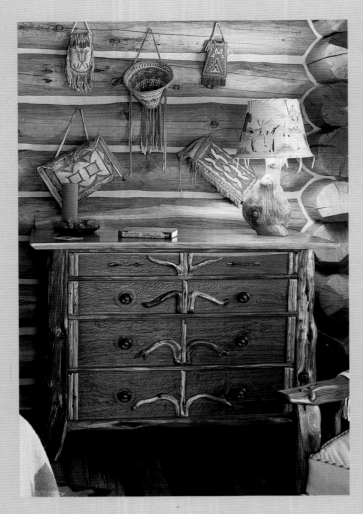

This extraordinary bureau made from walnut and juniper attests to artisan Jimmy Covert's attention to detail and his ability to create beautiful forms.

Classic western bureau, bed and mirror by New West.

The deer is a common motif in western rustic. The hardware on this bureau was cut from antlers and the top is covered with leather.

An entertainment center houses a small TV and other electronic gear at a Wyoming ranch. A poster of John Wayne guards the room when the owner's children are away.

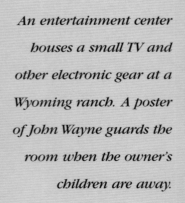

This entertainment center was constructed by Doug and Janis Tedrow of Ketchum, Idaho.

Built-in bunk beds are a favorite hiding spot for the children who sleep there.

Versatile lodgepole pine frames a freestanding full-length mirror.

A buffalo rug covers this bed, made by Ron and Jean Shanor from lodgepole pine branches.

Not all rustic settings offer rustic furniture. This master bedroom in a Montana log cabin is complete with period mahogany furniture.

A Scandinavian bed fits comfortably into this Montana log home.

A variety of Native American-influenced textiles cover this bed.

Longhorn steer horns occupy wall space above a western bed.

Stands of burled lodgepole pine, which are a favorite material for western rustic furniture makers, are often difficult to find. Burls, called an "excrescent" by wood professionals, are caused by disease, injuries, or stress to the trees.

Collaboration resulted in this ambient dining setting: table by Jimmy Covert, chairs by Lester Santos, and curtains by Lynda Covert.

The chair, lamp, and side table were built by Lester Santos, an accomplished musician and guitar builder. He creates one-of-a-kind pieces from his work-shop in Cody, Wyoming.

This set of furniture, made of lodgepole pine, is a western take on an Arts & Crafts design. The fire screen, table lamp, and other items are classic western accessories.

Michael Patrick of New West constructed this classic western furniture. Known as the most productive of all the western builders, Michael's furniture is well-designed, comfortable and sure to last for generations. Winner of numerous awards for his innovative designs, his furniture is frequently featured in magazines.

This counter was constructed with burls and native lodgepole pine, and the chairs are made of hickory. The built-in bookshelves provide space for the owner's extensive collection. Modern appliances occupy the opposite side of the counter.

Inspired by the furniture of Thomas Molesworth, Michael Patrick

designed this contemporary set.

Courageous colors and western textiles accent New West's

leather set in the tradition of Thomas Molesworth.

Furniture upholstered in natural colors blends well with log interiors. Home by Teton Heritage Builders, Eliot Goss.

This log home setting features a credenza and entertain-
ment center built in the style of the Reverend Ben Davis.
Doug and Janis Tedrow created the chip-carved pieces.

A rugged, rough-cut chair

is made comfortable by

several layers of textiles.

A contemporary bunkhouse in Wyoming is furnished with lodgepole pine bunk beds adorned with colorful bedding. The armchair is of classic gypsy design.

A child's bedroom in Aspen, Colorado, is given a contemporary western style with bunk beds, armchair and floor lamp by New West.

Doug Tedrow of Wood River Rustics
built this innovative sideboard
with willow molding.

This study, located in a small addition of a Montana log home,
houses a built-in desk constructed from antique barn boards. The
desk chair is by Old Hickory Furniture Company.

A balcony view of this home reveals a classic western chandelier and armchairs by Jimmy Covert.

Lodgepole pine shows off its design adaptability in a bureau by New West.

Rocky Mountain Juniper executed this ornate juniper bureau and table.

Arts & Crafts partners with western furniture in this impressive contemporary log home. The massive metal-and-glass chandeliers give off light that enhances the warm color of the logs.

Just what one might expect to see in a typically western-designed rustic room: a small desk made from locally cut pine trees, embellished with elk and mule deer antlers serving as the gallery and drawer pulls. The chair is woven with rawhide.

Lester Santos hand-carved this exquisite cherry headboard in traditional western motifs.

This classic western-influenced bed and related accessories complement the northern Rockies setting where they reside.

An original Thomas Molesworth
desk made in the 1930s.

The hand-carved panels of original western scenes make this desk by Lester Santos a work of art. The legs are juniper and the dimensional wood is cherry. The lampshades are lined with mica.

This library desk is located in the main room at the Crossed Sabres Ranch in Wyoming, where guests enjoy perusing the many vintage books and are delighted but not surprised to see grizzly bears wander in and out of the campgrounds. The lamp is hand-carved and is probably late Victorian. The chairs, dated earlier, are by Old Hickory Furniture Company.

Lester Santos is a master carver, as evidenced by the moose scene in the doors and drawers of this cupboard. A collection of antique Adirondack accessories completes the setting.

A rustic study center in Montana houses modern communication conveniences. The desk was made from old barn boards and locally cut branches.

John Gallis won an award at the 1999 Western Design Conference for this desk and chair.

Computer desk by Michael Patrick of New West.

Jimmy Covert made this impressive sideboard. His craftsmanship and innovation have brought him to the forefront of western design.

Detail of a cupboard by Lester Santos.

Boasting a hammered-copper top, this sideboard by Lester Santos in solid-cherry dimensional wood features a hand-carved scene on the doors. The table lamps are by Adirondack builder Tom Benware, and the original painting and frame were created by renowned artist Veronica Nemethy.

This high-end desk and chair set won the "Best of Show" award at the 1999 Western Design Conference. They were created by Ron and Jean Shanor of Wild Wood Furniture in Cody, Wyoming.

A variety of Native American collectibles enhance the western appeal of this desk and chair set, although the furniture pieces by Jimmy Covert stand on their own as fine works of art.

Front panel detail of Covert desk.

The study at the Crossed Sabres Ranch in Wapiti, Wyoming, has stood untouched since the 1930s.

Crystal Farm crafted both the console table using fallow-deer and elk antlers, and the mirror using mule-deer antlers.

Antler and Horn Furnishings

Antler furnishings did not have their advent in the twentieth century or in America. Historic castles in Scotland, Ireland, Switzerland, Germany and other European countries were full of antler chairs, settees, chandeliers, mirror frames, and wall hangings. These same castles also had other furnishings adorned with antlers, including beds, bureaus, desks, and cupboards.

In America, horn furnishings were first introduced during the Victorian period. Further, horn pieces often won awards at furniture exhibitions around the country. Constructed both in Texas and Chicago, such chairs were considered expensive and out of the financial reach of most Americans at that time. For instance, in 1890, chairs made from the horns of longhorn steers and upholstered with silk tapestry sold for $85. Deer-antler chairs upholstered with silk tapestry sold for $70. Today antique horn and antler furnishings are rare and pricey.

In today's world, nothing dies for the sake of antler furniture. All ungulates—including deer, moose and elk—shed their antlers naturally every winter and new ones immediately begin to grow. By fall the antlers have grown back to an even-larger size. Usually, dropped antlers are quickly eaten for their minerals by small animals such as mice and porcupines. But at the National Elk Wildlife Refuge in Jackson Hole, Wyoming, thousands of elk spend the winter. In the late spring both Boy Scouts and Girl Scouts collect the fallen antlers, which are then auctioned off to the highest bidders each Memorial Day weekend in the Jackson town center. The majority of antlers are sold to craftsmen, who, in turn, create all sorts of furnishings, sculptures, knife handles and carvings.

Crystal Farm created

this superbly crafted

armchair and lamp.

The glass top allows a clear view of the organic forms inherent in the mule-deer antlers that comprise this occasional table.

A 1920s to '30s vintage antler armchair by John Wurtz of Cody, Wyoming. Wurtz was known to have made a variety of furnishings, including armchairs and settees.

The artists at Crystal Farm made this oversized antler armchair.
Rich tapestry adds to the drama of the fallow-deer and elk-antler
chair, which is surprisingly comfortable.

This red-upholstered Victorian sofa is replete with horns and cow feet. Popular during the late 1800s, such pieces were made in Chicago and Texas. Settees of this type frequently won awards at national shows. Not surprisingly, such pieces are collected for their historical significance, style and design.

This audacious leather and moose-antler armchair was created by Dan MacPhail. His bold forms, quality and innovations have brought him significant recognition during the past several years.

A console table made from elk antlers is a focal point of this lush setting created by Steve Kent and Joan Benson of Crystal Farm.

154

The back side of the moose-antler wing chair by Dan MacPhail.

Dan MacPhail, who resides in Kentucky, built this massive wing chair, designing a fantastic piece of furniture from moose antlers, cowhides and leather.

156

Fallow-deer and mule-deer antlers adorn a bed
designed by Crystal Farm of Redstone, Colorado.

Another staircase project by Brent McGregor. The inclusion of free-form organic sculptural materials adds continuity to the entire project. Lights carefully applied to cavities on the reverse side of the wall-mounted sculpture make the sculpture glow in the evening.

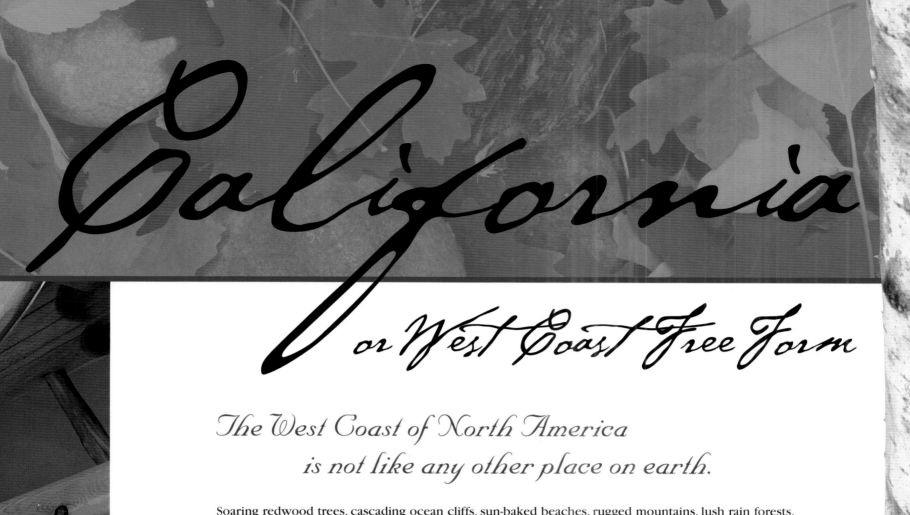

California

or West Coast Free Form

The West Coast of North America is not like any other place on earth.

Soaring redwood trees, cascading ocean cliffs, sun-baked beaches, rugged mountains, lush rain forests, and arid deserts have stirred creative expressions of all sorts. Inspired by a mild climate and a stunningly rich environment, individuals have been moved to create some of the most dramatic rustic furnishings ever produced.

Not for the faint of heart, California or West Coast "free-form" rustic furniture, along with rustic architectural embellishments, are often extreme in detail. Working with materials that lack the discipline of conformity and maintain a profound spirit of freedom and individuality, West Coast rustic furniture makers seek exaggerated examples in woods such as myrtle, twisted juniper, maple, redwood and other indigenous organic materials.

Brent McGregor, certainly one of the most accomplished of the free-form rustic artists, has created pieces from burls and stumps on trees that weighed over ten thousand pounds, requiring trucks and cranes to move both his materials and his artworks. "Big trees," McGregor says, "foster big imaginations."

Northern California and Oregon seem to have a preponderance of individuals working in the rustic medium. Driving down the highways in the redwood forests of northern California, one sees someone selling burls, whirligigs, rustic planters, sightseeing tours and rustic furniture at almost every commercial juncture. Slab-top tables and armchairs are most common, as are redwood chain-saw carvings.

The boldest and most expressive of the free-form artists use wildly contorted materials that speak deeply of the psychological and spiritual freedom so often associated with the West Coast. To the delight of both the artist and the consumer, California rustic abounds with absolute humor, grotesqueness, freedom and passion. Using materials deformed in every possible way, artists approach these cellulose maladaptations of nature and force viewers to confront passions often associated with terror and other primeval emotions. Hideous to some, it is this very truth that humanity finds inviting. Rustic furniture, and West Coast rustic in particular, addresses deep-seated turmoil often associated with the ravings of madmen. Through West Coast rustic, nature's most primitive calls—calls that are within all of us—are adapted to meet the inspired needs of both the artist and the art lover.

Rustic furniture draws us close to the inner fabric of ourselves and of nature. Hard-wired into our brains is the truth that for more than seven million years, or thirty-five million generations, we lived in the forests and in the trees. We fought great battles to survive and struggled against tremendous odds as a species to get to this point. Rustic furniture and rustic lifestyles are most profoundly influenced by our past. Rustic furniture makes no attempts to deceive anyone. It is natural in every way. You either love it or you hate it. There is no in-between. Civilization, with all its creations and artificiality, tries its best to negate the call of the wild. The beasts and monsters of our prehistoric past often raise their ubiquitous heads squarely in our lives and demand to be heard. Carl Sagan addressed this idea when he discussed why so many of us occasionally dream of falling: that for millions of generations while we lived in trees, that we might fall was our greatest fear. Freud also discussed these issues in much of his writings. He referred to such phenomena as "archaic remnants."

The limbic system, the oldest and most primitive area of our brains, offers us these dreams and nightmares and emotions. It is the seat of all passion in us. It is that part of our brain that has been with us since the beginning. We all have it, and it calls to us often.

Like their cousins in the Rocky Mountains, free-form rustic builders often work with burls, which are large bumps on trees resulting from reactions to insects, viruses, or injuries. In a way similar to how the human body responds to an insect bite, trees react by growing massive amounts of cellulose around the injury site. Larger trees such as maple and myrtle have burls that can grow to massive sizes and can eventually be made into tabletops or turned on a lathe into charming bowls or lampshades.

Burls, with their natural movement and freedom, captivate our imaginations. They add life to structure. Nature, they say, abhors a straight line. Human brains need change, and eyes are soothed and mystified when they find inherent motion. Living next to a beating rhythmic heart for the first nine months of our lives instills a sense of motion and rhythm in us; hence, the popularity of music and dance. Further, the motion and rhythm in nature captivate us. Naked trees in winter dance. Swaying and dancing in the winds, their arms and limbs mimic our veins and arteries. Their forms mystify us and yet we know that they are a part of us.

The twists, curves, and turns in branches are generally the tree's own actions to seek the nourishing rays of the sun. Called phototropism, this twisting of the branches is sensual in nature. Curvaceous and intoxicating, this bending speaks of passionate femininity.

Many builders on the West Coast collect driftwood that has been washed up on the shores by the ocean tides. They find materials left over from logging efforts; they may choose stumps of trees that were cut many years earlier. It is often necessary to dig the stumps out with a backhoe, remove them with a crane, and deliver them to the woodworker's shop on an eighteen-wheel flatbed truck.

Working with trees that are hundreds of years old, West Coast artists often take their inspiration directly from nature. Phil Clausen of Coquille, Oregon, makes the most distinctive and original mushroom-inspired lamps in the country. Matt Madsen and Tim Duncan of Orick, California, create beds, clocks, telephones, and other things that reflect the true nature of the materials with which they are working. In addition to their furniture, Brent McGregor and Kara Mickelson of Sisters, Oregon, often install huge sculptural trees inside contemporary rustic structures to bring nature indoors.

Tim Duncan and Matt Madsen made this queen-size bed. Solid and sturdy, the burled lodgepole pine bed is certain to last for generations.

Rustic supply yard of Brent McGregor and Kara Mickelson. The materials are mostly twisted juniper.

Ground-level view of a railing system created by Brent McGregor. Native organic materials such as leaves and moss were added to the trees to enhance the natural effect.

A grand staircase by Brent McGregor, created from twisted juniper, adds a sense of intrigue to this man's study.

To add high drama to a contemporary Washington home, Oregon rustic artist Brent McGregor installed two massive juniper trees in the entryway. Standing more than thirty feet tall, they astound visitors and architects alike.

Matt Madsen and Tim Duncan of Orick, California, built this rocking settee. The arms, legs, and stretchers were constructed from twisted juniper. The rockers are redwood, while the seat and back are maple.

"Big trees foster big imaginations"—and this thirty-foot-tall redwood stump is typical of the creative spirit often found in California rustic artists. Working with several different-sized chain saws, Raven Matthews creates colossal sculptures from the ancient carcasses of redwood trees.

Classic redwood rocker from Burl Art has a maple seat and back and a juniper frame. The chair is not only as sturdy as it appears but also amazingly comfortable.

Tall-case clock of juniper and maple burls by Matt Madsen and Tim Duncan of Burl Art in California. Using scrap materials often found along beaches and riverbanks, these two artists create organic pieces of art that typify the free-form movement.

Another view of McGregor's twisted-juniper pillars, which have been sandblasted to remove excess bark and other organic debris.

This massive floor lamp made by Phil Clausen stands nearly seven feet tall. The diameter of the shade, which is permanently fixed to the base, is four and a half feet. Constructed from myrtle and weighing more than three hundred pounds the lamp presently occupies a corner in the author's gallery and attracts considerable attention as clients marvel at its inherent humor and unique form.

Mounted on the outside of Phil Clausen's workshop is this extraordinary hand-carved lamp. Made from the stumps of ancient redwood trees, the lamp stands approximately twelve feet tall.

Exquisitely carved captain's chair, breakfast table, and table lamp from the studio of Oregon artist Phil Clausen. The pieces were created from maple.

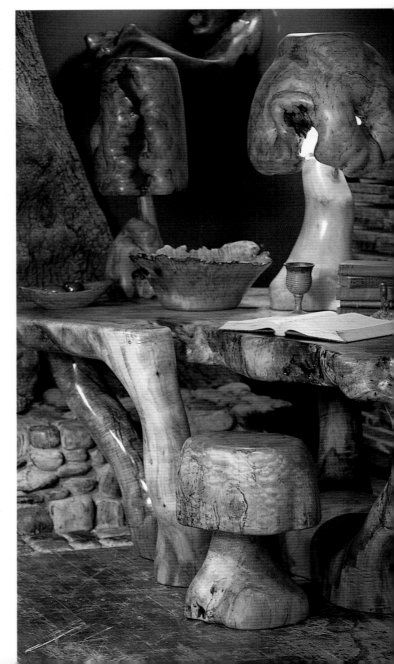

This desk and chair as well as the table lamp and bowl were fashioned by Phil Clausen.

Close-up view of McGregor's grand staircase. The entire project took three months to complete.

The entranceway to this grand Wyoming home is enhanced by the reintroduction of aspen trees to the immediate grounds. The massive logs create grandeur that matches the Teton Mountains, visible out the back windows of the structure that overlooks the Snake River.

Rustic from the Outside

An ideal rustic home is enchanting, inviting, and a little bit mysterious.

Porches should look like they have been there forever. There are plants, cats, dogs, birdfeeders, and a mailbox that matches the setting. There are old boots lined up and rich textiles scattered about. The house, nestled about with trees and vegetation, blends with the environment. Oversized rustic furniture on a cozy porch says, "Come sit on me." This ideal house invites you to kick off your shoes and watch the grass grow. An intriguing entryway beckons you to come inside. This is the place where families gather and where children play on rainy days. This is how communities stay together. Porches and entryways are the foundation of the home.

Rustic porches today are often embellished with branches that twist and bend in every direction imaginable. Inherently humorous, such material speaks of freedom, anarchy and chaos. It has followed its own calling and basically has done exactly what it has wanted to do in spite of the laws of nature. Along with this, after having given it some thought, many people are envious of the profound freedom inherent in nature. Nonetheless, in the hands of an accomplished rustic builder, such materials can blend perfectly with the immediate environment.

Further, many front porches have a rack of antlers crowning the entranceways. Such antlers will often fade in color with the years, but they always bring back stories of a great hunt or the day that they were found in a lonely corner of the woods.

Porches are casual. They're perfect for hot dogs and peanut-butter-and-jelly sandwiches. They also call for an occasional box of cookies (one should never feel guilty for occasionally consuming an entire box of chocolate-covered graham cookies and a quart of milk!) or a late-night slice of cold pizza. Porches are great places for naps and for lounging pets. But most of all, porches are places to relax and forget about the headaches of the world.

A Rocky Mountain cabin built in the 1930s has patinated to a classic dark color. The setting includes burls, antlers and rustic porch furniture.

Architect Jonathan Foote is best known for utilizing antique logs and other reclaimed building materials, as well as for his minimalist approach to design. This Rocky Mountain home blends perfectly with the immediate environment and maintains a classic historical look.

This stunning setting offers moose, elk, grizzly bears, coyotes, deer and the best trout fishing in America. Designed by architect Candace Tillotson-Miller and built from logs salvaged from local historical cabins, this Montana home is a tribute to creativity.

The entrance to this Montana home was constructed from stones and logs found on the property. Aspen trees were planted close to the house to retain the integrity and continuity of the environment.

Mankas Inverness Lodge in Inverness, California, is the setting for this cabin. Blending perfectly with the lush and mature environment, Mankas is known for its extraordinary four-star dining, its rich rustic environment, and its superb collections of rustic furnishings and accessories.

Located just south of Teton National Forest, this home blends naturally with the surrounding terrain. The large windows afford stunning views and allow the interior of the home significant passive solar heat and plenty of natural light to keep the electric bills down.

On the shores of a small lake in the Adirondacks, residents take the heavy snow in stride and enjoy a rich environment of cross-country skiing, ice fishing and skating just outside their back doors. A builder with foresight decided against cutting down all the trees when this cabin community was built.

What could be more inviting than being snow-bound in the Adirondacks with piles of new books and your favorite music? Although buried in winter snow, this Adirondack cabin maintains an inviting appearance.

The owner designed this classic Adirondack contemporary home. The upper facades of the structure are covered with white birch bark. The home blends ideally into the immediate environment.

Recycled vintage logs were the material for this home, where color and architecture blend confidently into the environment. The home was designed by architect Candace Tillotson-Miller and built by Yellowstone Traditions.

Stones for this small pond-side cottage were found on the property. While the main house sits on the hill directly behind it, the family uses the "fishing cottage" as a retreat and for quiet afternoons. The pond is full of monster rainbow trout.

Influenced by Victorian garden architecture, this charming gazebo was made from cedar by Romancing the Woods in Woodstock, New York. Known for their artistic detailing, Romancing the Woods has built such structures in many states.

Not only charming but convenient, this daily rental cabin in Alaska can be moved to any desired location by the renter.

Just outside of Denali National Park in Alaska, entrepreneurs took advantage of the log-home craze and completed a large number of log structures that cater to tourists.

Burls, furniture and plants give the porch a rustic ambiance.

This log cabin is for the birds!

This diminutive cabin is actually a children's playhouse. It is furnished with bunk beds and other fun accessories just right for kids.

This remarkable log cabin is an inspirational setting for an artist's office and workshop.

*An outdoor fireplace is used
frequently by the owners, who
enjoy afternoon cookouts.*

*This structure is actually the mailbox
for the Russell Creek Ranch, located just
outside of Yellowstone National Park.*

A tall settee built in the 1930s rests companionably on a front porch with an Old Hickory rocker from the same period.

Log "elbows" give this porch a sense of drama.

The owners of this Adirondack boathouse wanted a classic log cabin appearance, so they faced the building with log siding and used bark-off cedar trees and branches for the staircase, newel posts, banisters and railings.

The cabins at the historic Crossed Sabres Ranch just outside Yellowstone National Park were constructed with logs, huge burls for the porches, and plenty of antlers to adorn the cabin facades. The setting has remained untouched since the 1930s. A stay at this ranch is as peaceful as any on earth.

Located just south of Denali National Park in Alaska, this log cabin structure certainly falls into the folk art category.

This small cabin in Alaska is the home of a "flight seeing" company. With their pontoon planes positioned on a lake just outside their front door, the company does a brisk business in the tourist season. To help the cabins blend in with the environment, the company grows grass on the roof.

189

This ten-foot table can seat up to sixteen guests for a view of the Snake River in Wyoming. The setting is usually graced by passing wildlife.

Perched high on a Rocky Mountain bluff, this home blends perfectly with the fall colors of surrounding aspen trees.

Elk, grizzly bears, wolves, coyotes, eagles, mountain lions and deer are part of the habitat for this home designed by Jonathan Foote.

191

Adirondack builder Bruce Gunderson made this small shed. Bruce works primarily with bark-on cedar and builds innovative furniture and architectural elements.

This imaginative arm-chair presently resides on a patio in the Rocky Mountains of Colorado. The seat was made with leather strapping.

Built into this front porch are several benches that add to the ambiance and comfort of the home.

Stairs leading to this porch were made from old barn beams. Grass planted between the stairs gives the porch a "been there for years" feeling.

Doors

Doors are entities with several meanings. They can be closed to keep the warmth in and to secure one's self from the outside world. They can be opened to greet the world or passed through to allow entry to a completely new environment. They can be objects of beauty as well as mystery. "What's behind the door?" is a common question.

Rustic doors are inherently fun. They speak of forests and rugged lifestyles. They are not high-tech. There is no attempt to disguise the raw material. They are usually unpainted and always casual. They often have visible saw marks or ax marks on them, "honorable scars" that add to their rustic ambiance. They often have unusual hardware, with handmade wrought-iron, antlers, or branch handles making regular appearances.

They may be made of old barn boards or covered with twigs. They may be made with bark-covered logs. Old railroad ties make unique doors. Some doors have windows; some windows are made with stained glass. Some doors are carved with moose, bears, fish, trees, mountains or other rustic scenes. Perhaps they speak to us in "creaks and groans" when opened, claiming a life of their own.

Whatever the case, doors are always a threshold. They cover a passage to a new adventure. They provide safety and comfort as well as privacy. Doors let us relax and find time for ourselves. Whatever their orientation, they always say "welcome."

SUMMIT LAKE LODGE
ELEV. 1300

The birch-twig sideboard and armchair were made by Thome George of Washington. The back of the sideboard has been lined with white birch bark.

From the Inside

Living Spaces

Twigs, like the veins in our hands and the rivers of the land, dance and move to their own calling. Incorporated into furniture, twigs allow a three-dimensional view that can both intoxicate and thrill.

As best as can be surmised, twig furnishings first appeared in the Appalachian tourist regions late in the nineteenth century. There, wandering gypsies and other itinerants handcrafted rockers and tables from the young pliable shoots of willow, cherry, maple, hickory and other saplings. The furnishings were then loaded onto horse-drawn wagons and sold to lodges, hotels or anyone who was willing to either pay a price or accept a piece of work as payment for a meal.

Twig rockers, with their swirls and cascading lines, bear a resemblance to rockers and side chairs that were made in Vienna by the Michael Thonet company in and around the 1840s. Realistically, however, their exact evolution may never be known. Styles, individual peculiarities, and subtle innovations are a function of human whims and passions. Things are created and things are forever lost to the body of human knowledge.

In time, of course, the twig style (for lack of a better name) was embellished by individual craftsmen and eventually found its way to woodworkers throughout the Appalachian region, Pennsylvania, Ohio and Indiana. Because of its simplicity in form, materials and creation, the style eventually became extremely popular with Amish families across the East and into the Midwest. Today these historical chairs are considered very collectible, and numerous Amish families around the country fashion rockers, armchairs and side chairs, tables and a number of other furnishings from hickory shoots.

At the same time, a few craftsmen around the country have adopted twigs as their medium and are creating profoundly artistic variations on a theme that evolved during the 1800s. Certainly the two most influential individuals in the business of twig work are Clifton Monteith and Thome George.

A number of Monteith's creations on display in a Michigan museum.

This willow-sapling arm-chair is an example of the attention to detail and superb artistic form that make Clifton Monteith one of the most accomplished rustic artists in the country.

Clifton Monteith, of upstate Michigan, has been building twig chairs since 1985. A former illustrator from New York City, he is perhaps the most articulate of all the rustic furniture makers. Arguing that nature is neither digital nor quantifiable, Monteith refers to his rustic furniture making as a completely organic process. Using only green, undried materials, he strives for a cooperative synergy between all natural things. He adorns each aspen chair frame with willow shoots. His furnishings seem to flow and each piece maintains its own sense of movement. Recognized for his innovations, personal charisma and uncompromising pursuit of the artistic, Montieth has both tutored and mentored several up-and-coming rustic craftsmen.

Thome George, of Tonasket, Washington, has been building twig chairs since about 1990 and uses a variety of woods, including birch, hazel, serviceberry and other hardwoods in his creations. Influ-enced primarily by the art nouveau style, George's work is quite functional, innovative and extremely well made.

Although sweeping lines inherent in this armchair suggest an art nouveau or cubist influence, artisan Montieth argues that his shapes are inspired solely by naturally occurring organic forms found in wilderness settings.

An armchair made of birch saplings by Thome George exhibits the traditional Y back used by rustic furniture makers for decades. Cloudbird, George's partner in SweetTree Rustic, made the lamp and shade.

Bedside table by Thome George. He uses copper nails and traditional construction techniques in the creation of his artwork.

Veronica Nemethy's oil paintings reflect a classic Adirondack style.

This setting is located on a secluded island off the Washington State coast. Much of the material for this home was found as driftwood on the nearby beaches of the Pacific Ocean. The massive door is complete with stained glass.

This winding staircase leads up from a small study to the main section of the house. The stairs were constructed from antique barn boards.

This innovative setting includes a massive armchair by rustic artist John Omohundro.

Crystal Farm created this setting that includes the antler mirror. Located in Colorado, this company is known for its high-quality antler furniture and lush tapestries.

This small breakfast nook resides in a Rocky Mountain home. It overlooks mountains, rivers and fields, and the owners often enjoy passing moose and grizzly bears in their front yard.

An extraordinary side chair by rustic artist Randy Holden uses dried yellow birch saplings. Holden has created a chair that is innovative in design as well as functional.

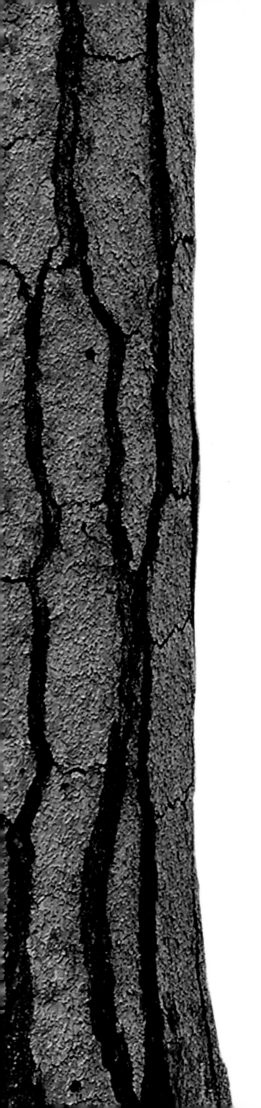

Made in the early 1900s, this classic Adirondack armchair includes hundreds of small hardwood twigs applied to a frame.

This close-up shows the detail
work of Adirondack builder
Jim Schreiner. Working with white
birch and hand-carved images,
Jim creates high-quality work
in the Adirondack tradition.

Detail work of Adirondack artist
Peter Winter. Using a variety of
woods, he has created many innovative pieces of furniture that grace
homes around the country.

Chris Wager created these innovative pieces of furniture from classic Adirondack materials. Although many rustic forms are organic in nature, these pieces incorporate geometric patterns that both enliven and accentuate the natural materials.

*This stove serves as a cock-
tail table at the UXU Ranch
in Wapiti, Wyoming.*

Fireplaces

A fireplace is the heart of the rustic home. For millions of generations people have gathered around fires for warmth and conversation. Ethereal to the point of fantasy, fire both captivates our imaginations and mystifies us. Fire is, in truth, nothing more than a dance of transformation. Capable of enchanting us into a trance, fire warms and calms us on cold winter nights.

Fires and fireplaces have been a part of human history since we first stood upright and took notice of the world in which we live. Archaeologists have reported fireplaces in the earliest homes in North America. Within the rustic setting, fireplaces have a critical role: they foster communication by getting us to turn off the TV, the plague of the modern era.

Fireplaces are often constructed with stones that are found on the property on which the home is built. Some fireplaces are massive monuments to our ability to build things big. Others are small and diminutive. Fires are also kept in ornate woodstoves. Whatever their origin, fireplaces and fires are often a necessity and always a gift.

The tools necessary to maintain a fire—andirons, grates, fire screens and mantels—have shown the creativity of rustic artists throughout the centuries. Fireplace elements often exhibit regional styles that depict such interesting scenes as wildlife and mountain scenery.

*This pot-bellied stove was used for
many years in Jackson, Wyoming.
Today such ornate stoves are considered to be stylish additions to
any rustic setting.*

The fireplace mantel and support logs were made from yellow birch trees. The ceiling in this room at the Lake Placid Lodge is lined with cedar bark.

This mantel for a fireplace at the Lake Placid Lodge was made by Peter Winter.

Historical buffalo andirons, probably from the 1920s. This pair resides in a classic log cabin owned by the State of Colorado.

A rare pair of swan andirons graces this fireplace in Colorado.

An ornate fire screen depicts a classic rustic moose-and-tree scene.

This mantel was completed with twisted juniper.

The fireplace has two sides. The side that faces the living room has a juniper mantel, and the other side, which faces a dining area, was completed with lodgepole pine.

This small stone cabin is a retreat on the shore of a trout-fishing pond in Montana. Complete with antique hickory furniture, the camp is a setting of peacefulness and comfort.

Twisted juniper fire-tool rack by Brent McGregor.

This fireplace setting is made more interesting by the incorporation of rustic accessories such as snowshoes, fishing creels and original paintings.

Although the structure that houses this fireplace is a Colorado log cabin, the interior furnishings and architectural elements speak of a Spanish influence.

This floor-to-ceiling fireplace was constructed in a Rocky Mountain home, where an old log cabin was torn down and rebuilt to meet the needs of the new owners.

A fireplace mantel at the Lake Placid Lodge was made of bark-on cedar.

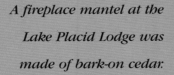

A twisted juniper log in the hands of artisan Brent McGregor became a uniqu[e] mantel.

Bathrooms

Bathrooms are the intimate rooms where we go to make ourselves look good and feel good. Bathrooms are private places. Parties are not usually held in bathrooms, except occasionally in bathtubs.

Rooms where we bathe tend to be small. We have a tendency to put hundreds of small items in bathrooms, so cabinets, shelves and drawers are always in short supply. In the past few years, designers and builders of rustic settings have started to pay attention to these bathing rooms. Consequently, the rooms have begun to acquire a sense of respectability.

Rustic bathrooms today are often made of old barn boards, wainscoting, rough-cut lumber and other organic materials. Designers have often included both American and European antique sinks and fixtures. Sink tops are occasionally made from old slate, granite, wide pine slabs and antique tiles. In warmer climates, an outdoor shower is often included for immediate relief from the heat.

One gentleman, against the wishes of his contractor and numerous others, included a two-hole privy in his personal bathroom. Others have used fossil stones, bricks and fieldstones to line the interiors of bathrooms. A few creative individuals have used the trunks of trees as the bases for sinks. Others have also used bark-off cedar poles to outline bathtubs and to add a touch of nature to the most private room in the house.

The vanity completed by Peter Torrance rests on a base that is a root stump from a yellow birch tree. Torrance has designed and constructed several of the finest homes in the Adirondacks.

Facilities at the Lake Placid Lodge include a shower for two and a sauna. The tub, also large enough for two, is within a few feet of Lake Placid. These are perhaps the finest rustic commercial facilities in the country, where one wakes to the sound of calling loons and ducks that like to be fed off the cabin's back porch in the morning.

This tub, which overlooks the Rocky Mountains in Wyoming, was made from small tiles and locally found stones. While relaxing in the tub, occupants enjoy the view of passing eagles and grizzly bears.

Barn boards and applied twigs make a bathroom statement.

A diamond-pattern mosaic dresses up the doors of a vanity made from vintage barn boards. Designer tiles on the backsplash make a colorful accent.

The cabinets in this tiny bathroom off a main entryway were constructed of aged barn wood and faced with a variety of locally cut branches. The corners of the cabinets are adorned with quarter-round lodge-pole burls.

Aged barn boards used for the cabinetry, mirror, and base for the tub are the prevalent construction material in this bathroom.

A cabin bathroom at the Lake Placid Lodge boasts a rustic look with a bark-off cedar vanity and applied birch bark on the walls and ceiling.

This tiny sink was constructed with stump-based lodgepole pine trees. Burls were added to the sides of the stand to complete the rustic appearance.

A heavily burled vanity and mirror give this small bathroom rustic ambiance.

Peeled cedar logs trim this bathtub, and small fieldstones give it a unique outline.

The walls of this bathroom are wainscoted in traditional Adirondack fashion. The large, sweeping branches are bark-off cedar.

229

The reverse side of white birch bark results in the dark color on this shade by Tom Benware.

Chandeliers and Lighting

Rustic chandeliers and lighting come in all shapes and sizes. Materials that were used in the past are often used today. Antlers are common and have been used for centuries. Initially antler chandeliers were constructed with small cups for holding candles. Today craftsmen run wires through the centers of drilled-out antlers and install electric sockets to complete the chandeliers. Most chandeliers are hung from ceilings and hot-wired to a control panel that regulates the brightness of the fixture.

For centuries, chandeliers have also been made from various metals. Often adorned with classic designs that were appropriate for the period and locale in which they were made, chandeliers are created for specific purposes and functions.

Chandeliers are also lined with a variety of materials. Glass has been a mainstay for the lighting industry for years. Made into a tremendous variety of patterns, glass in all shapes and colors has captured the fancy of builders and decorators alike. In the late 1890s, artists began using mica to line chandeliers, floor lamps and table lamps. Mica is mined from the ground, pressed into large sheets, and then cut into various shapes to meet the needs of the fixtures.

Numbers of rustic chandeliers have also been created from the natural contortions in wood. Chandeliers are occasionally created from the branches and roots of any number of trees. Chandeliers, sconces, table lamps and floor lamps have been created from burls that occur in many woods around the country. Humorous to the point of invoking laughter and delight, such lighting fixtures can contribute a very natural element to any setting and are always centerpieces of conversation.

A root-based table lamp crafted from a yellow birch tree stump. Yellow birch wood remains stable over the years, but white birch trees become unstable and are not used in the rustic furniture business.

Tips of mule-deer antlers are the material of this small table lamp, and the shade is chamois and rawhide.

Rustic artist Randy Holden
fashioned this floor lamp
from the roots and base of
a yellow birch tree. The
shade was made of white
birch. Acorns and pine-
cones embellish the piece.

One of three huge chande
liers, this one hangs fror
the ceiling of a modern lo
structure in Aspe
Colorado. The panels ar
glass and the motif incorpo
rates both western and late
Victorian stylin

Hides are another material that have been used in the lighting industry for years. Thomas Molesworth, in the 1930s, created a variety of chandeliers that incorporated hides. Many of these shades were also hand-painted with rustic western scenes. Craftsmen today are still using mica, glass and hides in their designs.

Several craftspeople are also making shades from the bark of birch trees. Difficult to work with, birch bark needs to be trimmed down thin before it will allow light to pass through. Nonetheless, birch-bark shades can offer a warm glow when correctly constructed. They are fragile, however, and will not handle abuse. At the same time, if a shade becomes damaged, it is easy to find a new piece of birch bark and sew it over the damaged area. Rustic furniture is not shy when it comes to repairs.

This Thomas Canada Molesworth deerskin chandelier (1930s) was hand-painted with traditional Native American motifs. It was exhibited for a time at the Buffalo Bill Historical Center in Cody, Wyoming, but its present home is the Pahaska Lodge (formerly owned by Buffalo Bill), just outside the east entrance to Yellowstone National Park.

Barney Bellinger created this chandelier out of a 1920s lamp base. He applied pinecones and roots from yellow birch trees for an organic element. The shades are hand-stitched rawhide.

Constructed of iron in the 1920s, this chandelier presently resides in a huge log structure owned by the State of Colorado. Its organic floral motif suggests late-Victorian origins. Originally created to hold candles, it was later electrified.

This chandelier presently hangs in the main lodge of the Crossed Sabres Ranch near Yellowstone National Park. The chandelier, which was created in the early 1930s from the burls of lodgepole pine, has mellowed to a rich warm color.

John Mortensen, of Wilson, Wyoming, made this western-motif chandelier. The panels of the lamp are mica, which was first introduced in the 1900s. The classical form of the chandelier suggests an art deco influence.

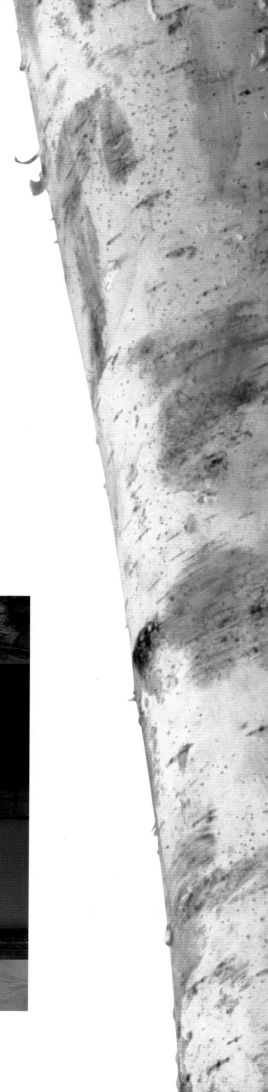

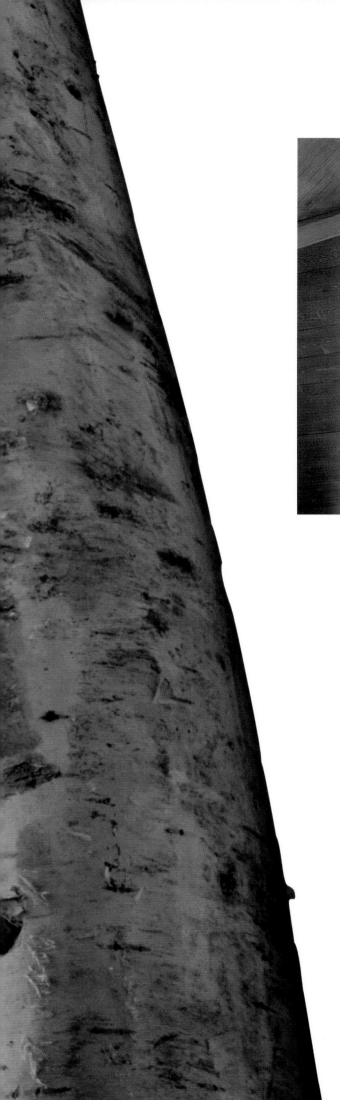

Lester Santos created this innovative chandelier. The wood is juniper and the panels on the shades are lined with mica.

Barney Bellinger adorned this chandelier, made from the stump of a yellow birch, with other organic elements, including acorns and pinecones.

This four-tier chandelier was created with both mule-deer and elk antlers.

The tavern at the Pahaska Tepee lodge is home to this small 1930s Thomas Molesworth chandelier.

This sconce was made by Barney Bellinger, who occasionally incorporates stones into his creations.

Cloudbird lined the shades of her sconce with rawhide and wrapped the arm with beads in traditional western motifs.

A small chandelier in a contemporary log home was made by New West of Cody, Wyoming.

An art deco– and western-influenced chandelier with mica panels is the creation of John Mortensen.

*Caribou-antler chandelier.
All ungulates, which
include deer, moose, elk,
and caribou, lose their
antlers annually, and
today's furnishings are
generally made from these.*

*This chandelier was made
with moose, elk and
fallow-deer antlers.*

Resources

Furniture Makers

Tony Alvis
Wilderness Iron Works
Taylor Ranch
1275 West Main
Ventura, CA 93001
(805) 648-2113
Tony is a blacksmith by profession and does custom work of chandeliers, gates, lighting, etc., in classical western as well as a variety of other styles.

Barney, Susan, and Erin Bellinger
Sampson Bog Studio
171 Paradise Point
Mayfield, NY 12117
(518) 661-6563
Barney Bellinger, certainly the best-known and most-sought-after rustic artist on the East Coast, is the quintessential rustic furniture maker. Often adorning his classical Adirondack pieces with museum-quality paintings, he works mostly with birch bark, and apples mosaic twig patterns to his furniture.

Dan and Steve Butts
High Country Designs
PO Box 5656
720 Main Street
Frisco, CO 80443
(970) 668-0107
(970) 668-4592 fax
E-mail: placer@colorado.net
Web site:
    www.highcountrydesigns.com
High Country Designs produces rustic furniture made from only the finest hand-selected indigenous materials.

Mark Catman
Birchbark Designs
47 Main Street
East Berne, NY 12059
(518) 872-9614
Mark works with birch bark to fashion traditional fishing creels, baskets, women's purses, and other high-quality Adirondack items.

Chris Chapman
Chapman Design
0075 Deer Trail Avenue
Carbondale, CO 81623
(970) 963-9580
(970) 963-0228 fax
Certainly the most accomplished leather worker today, Chris enjoys working in a variety of styles. Her pieces of furniture are adorned with high-relief leather scenes, and she often uses saddle leather bonded to a wooden framework for mirror frames, cabinetry, etc. During the last few years, she has won several awards at the Western Design Conference in Cody, Wyoming.

Stephen Chisholm
High Ridge Rustics
Stephen creates rustic furniture from a variety of New England woods, incorporating burls into his work.
    —before October 2000
58 Rowland Road
Old Lyme, CT 06371
(860) 434-6334
(860) 434-8058 fax
    —after October 2000
13 Old County Road
Waterford, VT 05848
(802) 751-8908

Phil Clausen
Clausen Studio
93937 Hwy 42 South at Riverton
Coquille, OR 97423
(541) 396-4806
Phil makes extraordinary furnishings from huge burls, specializing in all types of lamps up to 8 feet in height

and carved in a mushroom form. Many of his pieces, including dining room and coffee tables, are carved from single pieces of wood.

Diane Cole-Ross
Rustic Furniture
10 Cloninger Lane
Bozeman, MT 59718
(406) 586-3746
(406) 582-0844 fax
E-mail:
    webmaster@rusticfurniture.net
Web site: www.rusticfurniture.net
Diane builds custom furniture in classic western, Adirondack, and twig mosaic style.

Jimmy and Lynda Covert
Covert Workshops
2007 Public Street
Cody, WY 82414
(307) 527-5964 ph/fax
Jimmy and Lynda are two of the most respected western artists who work with furnishings and textiles. Jimmy builds one-of-a-kind pieces of furniture, and Lynda works with high-quality textiles to create a variety of custom-made products.

Marvin Davis and Robert O'Leary
Romancing the Woods, Inc.
33 Raycliff Drive
Woodstock, NY 12498
(914) 246-1020
(914) 246-1021 fax
E-mail: davis@rtw-inc.com
Web site: www.rtw-inc.com
Marvin and Bob are responsible for some of the finest cedar summerhouses and garden structures.

Jerry and Jessica Farrell
Box 255
Sidney Center, NY 13839
(607) 369-4916

Jerry Farrell works in the Adirondack style. He is best known for his extraordinary clocks and root pieces. Jessica often adorns Jerry's furniture with original paintings.

Peter Fillerup
Wild West Designs
PO Box 286
Heber, UT 84032
(435) 654-4151
(435) 654-1653 fax
E-mail: peter@wildwestdesigns.com
Web site: www.wildwestdesigns.com
Peter is a metalsmith who creates original lighting fixtures, furniture, sculptured metalwork, and bone china in a variety of designs. He is certainly one of the most respected artists within his medium.

Douglas Francis
Aurora Rustics
2054 Center Street
East Aurora, NY 14052
(716) 691-5600
E-mail: rfran85000@aol.com
Web site: http:\\members.aol.com\
    rfran85000.ar.html
Douglas creates fine handmade furniture and accessories in the rustic style from copper, stone, and contorted hardwoods, working primarily with peeled ironwood.

John Gallis
Norseman Designs West
38 Road 2AB
Cody, WY 82414
(307) 587-7777
John Gallis builds unique, one-of-a-kind functional pieces of furniture in designs of his own creation. His work is organic in nature with a refined western look. He uses walnut slabs in particular to fashion a variety of tabletops, desks, and chairs.

Thome George and Cloudbird
SweetTree Rustic
PO Box 1827
Tonasket, WA 98855
(509) 486-1573
Thome works with sticks and branches of birch and other native hardwoods, forming them into high-style chairs, cupboards, and sideboards. Cloudbird uses western materials and techniques to build beautiful lamps and lighting fixtures of her own design.

Glenn Gilmore,
    Architectural Blacksmith
Gilmore Metalsmithing Studio
PO Box 961
Hamilton, MT 59840
(406) 961-1861
E-mail: glenn@gilmoremetal.com
Web site: www.gilmoremetal.com
Glenn builds beautiful high-end "Art for the Hearth": fire screens, hearth tools, and other fireplace metalwork. He uses traditional and sculptural techniques to style metal furniture, fencing and gates, and one-of-a-kind custom pieces.

Tim Groth
PMB 158
111 Broadway, Ste 133
Boise, ID 83702
(208) 338-0331
(208) 424-0545 fax
Tim builds classical rustic furnishings of his own design. He has the utmost respect for Mother Nature and is environmentally conscious of the materials he selects.

Bruce Gundersen
PO Box 97
Keene, NY 12942
(518) 576-2015

Bruce has been building rustic furniture for many years. He works with bark-on cedar and offers custom pieces and traditional designs.

Chris Hawver
The Woodsmith
364 Hopkins Hill Road
Coventry, RI 02816
(401) 826-7321
Chris offers a line of affordable rustic furnishings, including tables, frames, and signs made in classic Adirondack style.

Hilary Heminway and Terry Baird
Montana Wagons
PO Box 1
McLeod, MT 59052
(406) 932-4350 or (860) 535-3110
Hilary and Terry refurbish sheep wagons, wall tents, and outhouses into unique rustic settings. Hilary was featured in the December 1999 issue of Architectural Digest *and its "100 Designers." She also decorates homes (see "Interior Decorators" on p. 248).*

Randy Holden
Elegantly Twisted
73 East Dyer Street
Skowhegan, ME 04976
(207) 474-7507
Randy is perhaps the most creative individual in the business. He works with birch bark in an Adirondack style that he alone created.

Michael Hutton
Twig Mosaic Creations
RR2 Box 162
Pittsfield, IL 62363
(217) 285-5277
E-mail: mphutton@adams.net
Web site: http:\\homepages.msn.com\
    CommercialSt\alicedad\surprise.html

Michael builds chairs and settees, applying original mosaic scenes to his furniture.

Wayne Ignatuk
Rustic Woodworks
55 Trumbulls Corner Road
Jay, NY 12941
(518) 946-7439
Wayne offers some of the finest furniture made in the Adirondacks today. He works with a variety of woods, including maple, yellow birch and other materials.

Amber Jean
1106 West Park #268
Livingston, MT 59047
(406) 222-9251
E-mail: amber@amberjean.com
Web site: www.amberjean.com
Amber Jean builds large pieces of furniture, including beds, chests, and gun cabinets, adorning her creations with a variety of hand-carved figures such as horses and wildlife. She is the winner of the 1999 Best Western Spirit and People's Choice awards at the Western Design Conference in Cody, Wyoming.

Stephen Kent and Joan Benson
Crystal Farm Antler Chandeliers
    and Furniture
18 Antelope Road
Redstone, CO 81623
(970) 963-2350
(970) 963-0709 fax
E-mail: cfarm@rof.net
Crystal Farm offers high-quality antler-themed chandeliers, lights, and furniture such as armoires and desks, including upholstered pieces. For example, lighting fixtures may feature hand-carved heads with attached antlers. Their work is quite unique.

Mike Kuba
PO Box 2560
Glens Falls, NY 12801
(518) 792-0160
E-mail: rusticchairwright@yahoo.com
Mike builds tables, cabinets, and large comfortable chairs from a variety of native woods. His specialty is making chairs with yellow birch.

Jack Leadley
Leadley's Adirondack Sugar Bush
PO Box 142
Speculator, NY 12164
(518) 548-7093
Jack Leadley builds the finest Adirondack rockers and pack baskets in the country. He, himself, is a classic.

Dan MacPhail Antler Studio
1645 McKendree Church Road
Kevil, KY 42053
(270) 488-2522
E-mail: bear@apex.com
Dan builds original, unique, high-quality antler chairs, chandeliers, and other furnishings.

Brent McGregor & Kara Mickelson
Rocky Mountain Timber Products
Box 1477
Sisters, OR 97759
(541) 549-1322
Brent and Kara offer a completely original perspective to the rustic furniture business. With years of background in the rustic tradition, they build a full line of home furnishings, often adorning structures with unique architectural elements.

Matt Madsen and Tim Duncan
Burl Art Productions
PO Box 187
Orick, CA 95555
(707) 488-3795
(707) 488-3565 fax

E-mail: burlart@juno.com

Matt and Tim work together to create original, free-form California furniture made from a variety of California and Oregon woods.

Lionel Maurier

Rustic Renditions
26 Tucker Mountain Road
Meredith, NH 03253-9627
(603) 279-4320 ph/fax

Lionel custom-designs and builds traditional high-quality rustic and new-transitional Adirondack-style furniture, working with a variety of woods.

Clifton Monteith

PO Box 9
Lake Ann, MI 49650
(231) 275-6560 ph/fax
E-mail: monteithc@aol.com

Clifton is an artist in the truest sense. He makes original furniture out of willow shoots, and has refined his style of rustic furniture into classic new designs.

John Mortensen

The Rainbow Trail Collection
PO Box 746
Wilson, WY 83014
(307) 733-1519
(307) 733-5216 fax
E-mail: mortensen@rmisp.com
Web site: www.mortensenstudios.com

Using foundry castings with each piece he makes, John builds rustic furniture, chandeliers and other lighting fixtures in the traditional western fashion.

Nick Nickerson

PO Box 618
Copake, NY 12516
(518) 329-1665

Nick offers high-quality picture frames of original designs.

Old Hickory Furniture Company

403 South Noble Street
Shelbyville, IN 46176
(317) 392-6740
(800) 232-2275 toll-free
(317) 398-2275 fax
E-mail: mail@oldhickory.com
Web site: www.oldhickory.com

Old Hickory is the largest and oldest of the commercial builders in the country. They offer hundreds of different designs as well as custom items.

John Omohundro

Freeflowing Design
3765 South 19th
Bozeman, MT 59718
(406) 585-2699
E-mail: johnyo2@yahoo.com

John builds free-form furniture, including tables and chairs, in unique designs. He also does installation and embellishment pieces in the home.

J. Mike Patrick

New West
2811 Big Horn Avenue
Cody, WY 82414
(307) 587-2839
(800) 653-2391 toll-free
(307) 527-7409 fax
E-mail: newwest@trib.com
Web site: www.newwest.com

Mike offers a complete selection of contemporary and traditional western furnishings as well as Molesworth-inspired designs. He is the winner of numerous awards.

Robby Porter

Deadwood Design
Box 65
Adamant, VT 05640
(802) 223-2153
E-mail: portershop@aol.com
Web site: www.robbyporter.com

Robby creates high-end beds, lamps, chairs, bureaus and other furniture from local woods, focusing on free-form style but with simple, clean lines.

Andy Sanchez

Custom Furniture by Andy Sanchez
205 South Main Street
Belen, NM 87002
(505) 864-2003 ph/fax
(888) 212-7722 toll-free
E-mail: sanchez9@compuserve.com
Web site: www.specialtymile.com\
customfurniture

As a relative newcomer to the field, Andy builds very unique, high-quality furnishings inspired by traditional western and Native American motifs. The juniper wood he uses is between 500 and 1,400 years old; he also mixes marble and other stones with his work.

Lester Santos

Santos Furniture Company
2208 Public Street
Cody, WY 82414
(307) 587-6543
(888) 966-3489 toll-free
(307) 527-4407 fax
E-mail: lester@santosfurniture.com
Web site: www.santosfurniture.com

Lester, the winner of numerous awards, creates high-quality original furniture in the western tradition.

Jim Schreiner

PO Box 1407
Lake Placid, NY 12946
(518) 523-7081

Jim constructs high-quality rustic furnishings in the Adirondack tradition.

Ron and Jean Shanor
Wildewood Furniture Company
PO Box 1631
Cody, WY 82414
(307) 587-9558
(877) 208-4524 toll-free
(307) 527-7247 fax
Ron and Jean won the Best in Show award at the 1999 Western Design Conference in Cody, Wyoming. They create high-quality custom furniture of their own design.

Doug and Janis Tedrow
Wood River Rustics
PO Box 3446
Ketchum, ID 83340
(208) 726-1442
(208) 726-1430 fax
Doug and Janis build furniture inspired by nature. Working with native woods, they offer custom-made rustic furniture of the highest quality

Lori Toledo
318 West State Street
Johnstown, NY 12095
(518) 762-4462
Lori builds original, unique picture frames in classical Adirondack style.

Chris Wager
205 Riceville
Gloversville, NY 12078
(518) 661-6697
Chris works in the traditional Adirondack style. He builds one-of-a-kind, high-end rustic furnishings.

Judd Weisberg Designs
Route 42 Box 177
Lexington, NY 12452
(518) 989-6583 ph/fax
E-mail: aware@mhonline.net
Judd builds high-quality, custom-made furniture, including tables,

mirrors, and beds, with driftwood and other select northeastern woods. He deals primarily in commissioned work.

Tom Welsh
The Rustic Homestead
PO Box 68
Minerva, NY 12851
(877) 251-4038 toll-free
(518) 251-0800 fax
Tom fashions high-end rustic furniture, specializing in chairs of yellow birch and maple, with contoured wooden seats and backs.

Norman West
Spirit of the West Log Furniture
C-238
108 Ranch, BC V0K 2Z0
Canada
(250) 791-5793
Norman builds chairs, tables, frames, mirrors, and a variety of other furnishings with deadwood, including diamond willow, juniper, black sage, and antique fir.

Home Builders

Peter Torrance
Torrance Construction
Cascade Road
Lake Placid, NY 12946
(518) 523-3225
Peter acts as designer, architect and contractor and has built many of the finest and most innovative homes in the Adirondacks.

Yellowstone Traditions
PO Box 1933
Bozeman, MT 59771
(406) 587-0968
This company is certainly one of the great construction companies in the West. They have been in business many years and have constructed some of the greatest western homes I've ever seen.

Interior Decorators

Diana Beattie Interiors
1136 Fifth Avenue
New York, NY 10128
(212) 722-6226
(212) 722-6229 fax
E-mail: dianabeattieint@aol.com
and
P.O. Box 193
McAllister, MT 59740
(406) 682-5700
(406) 682-5701 fax

Barbara Collum
  Decoration and Design
6976 Colonial Drive
Fayetteville, NY 13066
(315) 446-4739 ph/fax
E-mail: bmctpc@mindspring.com

Kari Foster
Associates III
1516 Blake Street
Denver, CO 80202
(303) 534-4444
(303) 629-5035 fax
E-mail: assoc3@aol.com

Cheryl Gallinger
Gallinger Trauner Designs, Inc.
3785 South Lake Creek Drive
Wilson, WY 83014
(307) 733-0902 / 733-0970
(307) 733-0935 / 733-9302 fax

Melissa Greenauer
Greenauer Design Group, Inc.
PO Box 5963
Vail, CO 81658
(970) 926-1783
(970) 926-1784 fax
E-mail: melissag@colorado.net
Web site: www.greenauer.com

Hilary Heminway
140 Briarpatch Road
Stonington, CT 06378
(860) 535-3110
(860) 535-4546 fax

Architects

Michael Bird, AIA
Adirondack Design
77 Riverside Drive
Saranac Lake, NY 12983
(518) 891-5224
(518) 891-5227 fax
E-mail: mbird@adkgreatcamps.com
Web site: www.adkgreatcamps.com

Camens Architectural Associates, AIA
    Barry Halperin, architect
    Michael Reynolds, designer
126 West Main Street
Malone, NY 12953
(518) 483-1585
(888) 821-6930 toll-free
(518) 483-1746 fax
E-mail: cagcad@northnet.org

Candace Tillotson-Miller, Architect
PO Box 467
Livingston, MT 59047
(406) 222-7057
(406) 222-7372 fax

Peter Dominick
The Urban Design Group, Inc.
1621 - 18th Street, Ste 200
Denver, CO 80202
(303) 292-3388
(303) 292-6574 fax
E-mail:
    pdominick@urbandesigngroup.com
Web site: www.urbandesigngroup.com

Jonathan L. Foote and Associates
126 East Callendar
Livingston, MT 59047
(406) 222-6866
(406) 222-6869 fax
E-mail: jlf@jlfarchitects.com
Web site: www.jlfarchitects.com

Galleries

George Albright
209 SE 15th Avenue
Ocala, FL 34471
(352) 620-0750
(352) 620-2363 fax
Web site: www.rusticonline.com
George sells high-end rustic antiques.

Sharon Boucher
Avalanche Ranch
12863 Hwy 133
Redstone, CO 81623
(970) 963-2846
(877) 963-9339 toll-free
(970) 963-3141 fax
E-mail: aranch@rof.net
Web site: www.avalancheranch.com

Avalanche Ranch offers a large selection of antique and collectible rustic furnishings and accessories, including primitive work, textiles, blankets and rugs, and sports memorabilia such as skis, snowshoes, fishing gear, and accessories.

Henry Caldwell
Black Bass Antiques
PO Box 788
Main Street
Bolton Landing, NY 12814
(518) 644-2389
(518) 644-2047 fax
E-mail: hacantique@aol.com
Web site: www.blackbassantiques.com
Black Bass Antiques features a wide selection of antique rustic accessories, including boats and fishing gear.

Thom Heil and Paula Jenkins
Rustic Comforts
120 Main Street
Milford, OH 45150
(513) 965-8944 ph/fax
Web site: www.rusticcomforts.com
Rustic Comforts offers a good selection of rustic furniture and accessories, specializing in Woolrich and Pendleton blankets as well as Old Hickory Furniture.

Ralph Kylloe Gallery
PO Box 669
Lake George, NY 12845
(518) 696-4100
E-mail: rkylloe@capital.net
Web site: www.ralphkylloe.com
This gallery features the country's largest selection of rustic furnishings, antique rustic accessories, and antler chandeliers by many of the artists featured in this book, and provides complete custom work for rustic furnishings.

Marty Kruzich and Ron Harris
Martin-Harris Gallery
60 East Broadway
Jackson, WY 83001
(800) 366-7814
(307) 734-1100 fax
E-mail: martykruzich@jhinet.com
     or pamwinters@jhinet.com
The Martin-Harris Gallery features a large selection of contemporary western furnishings, including one-of-a-kind paintings and sculpture pieces.

Bob and Judy Oestreicher
Moose America Antiques
97 Main Street
Rangeley, ME 04970
(207) 864-3699 ph/fax
(603) 431-9765 ph/fax
E-mail: bobmemoose@mediaone.net
Moose America offers a good selection of antique rustic accessories.

Hank and Robert Ross
Ross Bros.
28 North Maple Street
Florence, MA 01062
(413) 586-3875
E-mail: mail@rossbros.com
Web site: www.rossbros.com
This antiques dealership also offers the country's largest selection of outdoor equipment, including antique canoes, boats, and related accessories.

Terry and Sandy Winchell
Fighting Bear Antiques
PO Box 3790
375 South Cache Drive
Jackson, WY 83001
(307) 733-2669 ph/fax
Terry and Sandy deal in a variety of styles such as early Mission, and offer the country's most extensive selection of antique Molesworth furnishings and accessories. They also sell antique Old Hickory and native lodgepole.

Material Sources

Ollie Burgess
Specialty Wood Products, Inc.
Mill Street
Bloomingdale, NY 12986
(518) 891-9149 / 891-5815
(518) 891-2311 fax
Ollie sells birch bark, yellow birch, and other Adirondack woods for furniture and architectural applications. He also makes custom log railings.

Hank Ingram
Box 2552
Cody, WY 82414
(307) 527-7462
E-mail: ingram@myavista.com
Web site: www.burlweb.com
Hank sells burls, lodgepole pine, juniper, and other Rocky Mountain woods.

Marty McCurry
Highland Craftsmen
PO Box 2011
151 Pine Street
Blowing Rock, NC 28605-2011
(828) 295-0796
E-mail: highlandcraftsmen@boone.net
Web site: www.highlandcraftsmen.com
These folks not only provide bark for home siding but also offer architectural detailing such as banisters, railings, staircases, and other embellishments.

Northern Hardwoods
PO Box 308
Lake George, NY 12845
(518) 668-4501
Tom and Don Devlin sell some of the finest and most in-demand furniture-grade woods in the country. This place is a woodworker's heaven.

Chair Weavers

Vito Decosmo
23 Westview Drive
Belchertown, MA 01007
(413) 323-7224

Vito is an expert East Coast chair weaver and repairman. He includes caning, weaving, and fiber rush in his work, and uses a variety of weaving patterns—herringbone, diamond, and Indian, to name a few.

Kathi Pruitt
The Bane of Old Cane
4331 East Mahalasville Road
Morgantown, IN 46160
(812) 597-2440
Kathi can professionally re-weave or re-cane any chair ever made.

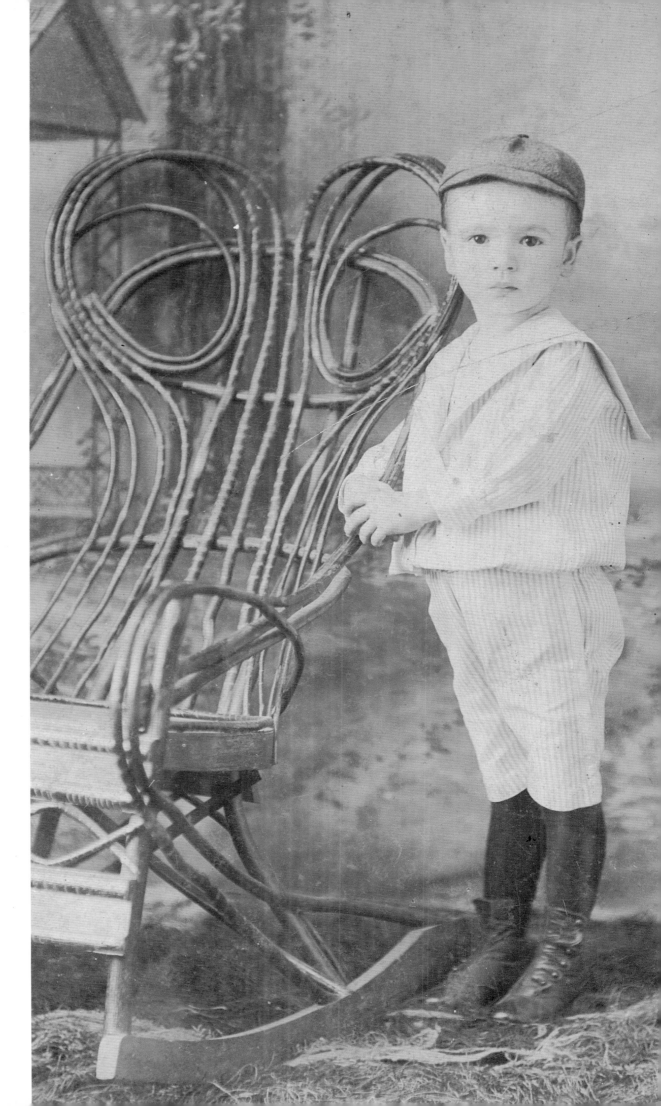

Index

Adams, Michael, 56
Adirondack Design, 249
Albright, George, 249
Alvis, Tony, 244
Amber Jean, 246
Associates III, 248
Aurora Rustics, 36, 245.
    See also Francis, Douglas
Avalanche Ranch, 249

Baird, Terry, 246
Bane of Old Cane, The, 251
Barbara Collum Decoration and Design, 248
Beattie, Diana, 248
Bellinger, Barney, 17, 55, 65, 244;
    desk, 24–25; paintings, 24, 34, 40, 59,
    67, 205; table, 37, 56, 60, 68; sideboard,
    38; lighting, 38, 234, 238, 240; mirror, 38,
    60; chest, 40; studio, 44–45;
    furniture, 49; cupboard, 53, 62; bed, 56;
    artwork, 67; setting, 69
Bellinger, Erin, 65, 244
Bellinger, Susan, 25, 65, 244
Bennett, John, 17, 56, 60
Benson, Joan. *See* Crystal Farm
Benware, Tom, 16, 17; cupboard, 38;
    table, 56; lamps/shades, 60, 145, 231;
    sideboard, 71
Birchbark Designs, 244
Bird, Michael, AIA, 249

Black Bass Antiques, 249
Boswell, Al, 17
Boucher, Sharon, 249
Burgess, Ollie, 250
Burl Art Productions, 165, 246–47
Butts, Dan and Steve, 244

Caldwell, Henry, 249
Camens Architectural Associates, AIA, 249
Candace Tillotson-Miller, Architect, 249
Catman, Mark, 244
Champney, John, 24
Chapman, Chris, 17, 95, 244
Chisholm, Stephen, 26, 66, 244
Clausen, Phil, 17, 160, 244–45; lamp, 162,
    166, 170; chair/table, 170; desk, 170
Cloudbird, 241, 245
Cole-Ross, Diane, 17, 90, 245
Collum, Barbara, 248
Covert, Jimmy, 17, 245; settee, 99; table, 106,
    125; bureau, 118; chandelier, 136; chairs,
    136, 146; sideboard, 144; desk, 146
Covert, Lynda, 125, 245
Crystal Farm Antler Chandeliers and
    Furniture: living room set, 98; table, 148,
    154; mirror, 148, 208; chair, 149, 152;
    lamp, 149; setting, 154–55; bed, 157,
    208; location, 246
Custom Furniture by Andy Sanchez, 247

Dan MacPhail Antler Studio, 246
Davis, Marvin, 245
Deadwood Design, 247
Decosmo, Vito, 251
Diana Beattie Interiors, 248
Dominick, Peter, 249
Duncan, Tim, 17, 160, 161, 164, 169,
    246–47. *See also* Burl Art Productions

Elegantly Twisted, 246

Farrell, Jerry, 17, 43, 51, 67, 245
Farrell, Jessica, 67, 245
Fighting Bear Antiques, 250
Fillerup, Peter, 245
Foote, Jonathan, 174, 191, 249
Foster, Kari, 248
Francis, Doug, 30, 36, 52, 245
Freeflowing Design, 247

Gallinger-Trauner Designs, Inc., 93, 249
Gallis, John, 17, 102, 104, 111, 143, 245
Garrett, David, 20
George, Thome, 17, 201, 203, 245; sideboard,
    200; chair, 200, 204; table, 204

Gilmore, Glenn, 245
Goss, Eliot, 130
Greenauer Design Group, Inc., 249
Groth, Tim, 17, 112, 245
Gunderson, Bruce, 192, 245–46

H

Halperin, Barry, 249
Harris, Ron, 250
Hawver, Chris, 246
Heil, Thom, 250
Heminway, Hilary, 246, 249
High Country Designs, 244
High Ridge Rustics, 244
Highland Craftsmen, 250
Holden, Randy, 17, 246; armoire, 23;
     lamp, 34, 232; sideboard, 36, 61;
     cupboard, 57; bureau, 62; sofa, 70;
     door hardware, 70, 71; chair, 210
Howard, Jim, 17, 29, 42, 63
Hutton, Michael, 17, 51, 68, 246

I

Ignatuk, Wayne, 17, 246
Imbs, Peter, 91
Indiana Hickory Furniture Company, 75
Indiana Willow Products Company, 75, 86
Ingram, Hank, 250

J

Jean, Amber, 246
Jenkins, Paula, 250
Jonathan L. Foote and Associates, 249
Judd Weisberg Designs, 248

K

Kelly, Brian, 17, 24, 63
Kent, Steve. *See* Crystal Farm

King, Don, 90
Kruzich, Marty, 250
Kuba, Mike, 31, 246
Kylloe, Ralph: home, 33, 53, 54, 60–61;
     design, 48, 52, 76–77; Gallery, 250

L

Lanthier, Jim, 42
Leadley, Jack, 17, 246

M

Mack, Dan, 16, 17
MacPhail, Dan, 17, 154, 156, 246
Madsen, Matt, 17, 160, 161, 164, 169, 246–47.
     See also Burl Art Productions
Martin-Harris Gallery, 250
Matthews, Raven, 164
Maurier, Lionel, 59, 247
McCurry, Marty, 250
McGregor, Brent: staircase, 158–59, 163,
     167, 171; of Oregon, 160–61, 246;
     pillars, 167, 168–69; fire-tool rack, 220;
     mantel, 222
Mickelson, Kara, 160–61, 246
Montana Wagons, 246
Monteith, Clifton, 16, 17, 201–3, 247
Moose America Antiques, 250
Mortensen, John, 236, 242, 247
Mowry, Tim, 109

N

Nemethy, Veronica, 22, 32, 41, 45,
     64, 145, 213
New West: dining room set, 101, 102;
     chair, 103; sofas, 113; sideboard, 106;
     table, 109; bedroom set, 118, 133;
     leather set, 129; bureau, 137;
     chandelier, 242; location, 247.
     See also Patrick, J. Michael

Nickerson, Nick, 247
Norseman Designs West, 245
Northern Hardwoods, 250

O

O'Leary, Robert, 245
Oestreicher, Bob and Judy, 250
Old Hickory Chair Company, 73
Old Hickory Furniture Company, xi, 21,
     72–86, 247; furniture, 28–29; chairs, 38,
     72, 134–35, 141; rocker, 187
Old Hickory Furniture
     (Shelbyville, Indiana), 48
Omohundro, John, 17, 107, 206, 247

P

Patrick, J. Michael, viii–ix, 17, 102, 127,
     128, 143, 247. *See also* New West
Porter, Robby, 247
Pruitt, Kathi, 250

R

Race, Greg, 102
Rainbow Trail Collection, The, 247
Ralph Kylloe Gallery, 250
Reynolds, Michael, 249
Rocky Fork Furniture, 88
Rocky Fork Juniper, 91, 97, 109
Rocky Mountain Juniper, 137
Rocky Mountain Timber Products, 246
Romancing the Woods, 181, 245
Ross Bros. (Hank and Robert), 250
Rustic Comforts, 250
Rustic Furniture, 245
Rustic Hickory Furniture Company, 77
Rustic Homestead, The, 248
Rustic Renditions, 247
Rustic Woodworks, 246

S

Sampson Bog Studio. *See* Bellinger, Barney
Sanchez, Andy, 17, 247
Santos, Lester, 17, 247; settee, 99; chairs, 102, 112, 125, 126; lighting, 126, 237; table, 126; headboard, 138; desk, 140; cupboard, 142, 144; sideboard, 145
Schreiner, Jim, 35, 212, 247
Shanor, Jean, 110, 122, 145, 248
Shanor, Ron, 17, 94, 108, 122, 145, 248
Skenandore, Rodney, 106
Specialty Wood Products, Inc., 250
Spirit of the West Log Furniture, 248
SweetTree Rustic. *See* Cloudbird; George, Thome

T

Tedrow, Doug and Janis, 17, 248; sideboard, 111, 134, 145; cupboard, 116, 117; entertainment center, 119, 131; credenza, 131
Teton Heritage Builders. *See* Goss, Eliot
Tillotson-Miller, Candace, 175, 180, 249
Toledo, Lori, 17, 60, 248
Torrance, Peter, 39, 223, 248
Twig Mosaic Creations, 246

U

United Crafts, 35
Urban Design Group, Inc., The, 249

W

Wager, Chris, 17, 41, 213, 248
Weisberg, Judd, 58, 248
Welsh, Tom, 17, 30, 248
West, Norman, 248
Wild West Designs, 245
Wilderness Iron Works, 244
Wildewood Furniture Company. *See* Shanor, Jean; Shanor, Ron

Winchell, Terry and Sandy, 250
Winter, Peter, 17; cupboard, 25, 27, 35; breakfront, 34; table, 37, 48; buffet, 48; bed, 53; twig work, 212; mantel, 216
Wood River Rustics. *See* Tedrow, Doug and Janis
Woodsmith, The, 246

Y

Yellowstone Traditions, 102, 180, 248

Other Books by Ralph Kylloe

Indiana Hickory Furniture (1988)

Indiana Hickory Furniture Makers (1989)

Rustic Traditions (1993)

Rustic Furniture Makers (1995)

A History of the Old Hickory Chair Company (1995)

Fishing Camps (1996)

Rustic Garden Architecture (1997)

Rustic Style (1998)

Cabin Collectibles (2000)

Picker (a novel, 2000)